all*you

EAT WELL, SAVE BIG

Cookbook

Have dinner with us!

What makes a perfect supper? It has to be quick and easy to make. It must be healthful, balanced and full of essential nutrients. Most importantly, it should taste great, be lip-smackingly satisfying and please everyone. Does such a thing exist? Absolutely! And it doesn't have to cost an arm and a leg, either. Welcome to the ALL YOU *Eat Well, Save Big Cookbook,* where we share 148 of our favorite suppers—all delicious, family-pleasing meals that cost less than $2.50 per serving. Enjoy!

Beth Lipton
Food Editor, ALL YOU

BE AN EXPERT

✳ **Make our easy recipes even simpler with these handy guides to often-used tools, techniques and ingredients.**

17 Prep chicken breasts for cooking

35 Keep food fresher and tastier longer

67 Chop onions like a pro

79 Keep dried spices tasting fresh

95 Chop herbs with ease

113 Keep cast iron in tip-top shape

133 Make perfect pasta

147 Prep an avocado with ease

153 Peel tomatoes effortlessly

169 Know your eggs

Contents

Chicken and Turkey 4

Beef and Lamb 54

Pork 82

Fish 124

Vegetables 134

The unexpected ingredient
that makes these drumsticks
(page 35) so tasty is coffee!

Chicken and Turkey

It's no secret that chicken and turkey make wonderful dinners. Poultry is versatile, family-pleasing and inexpensive—the trick is finding recipes that are easy and quick but break you out of the "Chicken, again?" rut. These dishes are tasty and filling without costing you extra time or money.

6 Herb-Parmesan Chicken Breasts
7 Chicken Thighs with Spicy Peanut Sauce
8 Easy Broiled Drumsticks
9 Slow-Cooker Barbecue Turkey Meatballs
11 Lemon-Rosemary Chicken
11 Spicy Chicken Stew
12 Cheesy Chicken Taco Casserole
13 Grilled Chicken Quesadillas
14 Caribbean Jerk Chicken
15 Chicken with Herbed Dumplings
17 Ricotta-and-Ham-Stuffed Chicken Breasts
18 Teriyaki Chicken Drumsticks
19 Turkey Reubens
20 White Bean and Chicken Chili
21 Turkey Cutlets with Fresh Corn
23 Chicken Salad Club Sandwiches
23 Chicken Piccata
24 Lemon-Herb Chicken Thighs
25 Braised Chicken with Potatoes
26 Corn Flake–Crusted Chicken
27 Turkey Meatballs
29 Grilled Chicken, Peach and Arugula Salad
29 Chicken Sausages with Beans
30 Turkey Nachos

31 Pasta with Chicken and Artichokes
32 Chicken Burritos
33 Chicken Breasts with Peppers
35 Coffee-Brined Chicken Drumsticks
36 Grilled Turkey, Cheddar and Apple Sandwiches
37 Chicken with Tomatoes and Arugula
38 Risotto with Turkey Sausage
39 Stuffed Summer Squash
41 Chicken Thighs with Mustard-Citrus Sauce
41 Asian Sesame Noodles with Chicken
42 French Bread Pizzas
43 Cheesy Twice-Baked Potatoes
45 Beer Can Chicken
45 Baked Potatoes Stuffed with Turkey, Bacon and Cheddar
46 Skillet Chicken Parmesan
47 Lemony Chicken Breasts with Rice
48 Curried Chicken and Chickpea Stew
49 Tortilla Soup
51 Creamy Chicken and Broccoli Curry
51 Crunchy Pecan-Crusted Chicken Fingers
52 Buttermilk Chicken Tenders
53 Chicken Fried Rice with Vegetables

Herb-Parmesan Chicken Breasts

Prep: 15 min.
Cook: 15 min.
Serves: 4
Cost per serving:

$2.07

- 1 tsp. grated lemon zest
- 1 small clove garlic
- ½ cup loosely packed parsley leaves
- 4 6-oz. boneless, skinless chicken breast halves
- Salt and pepper
- 1 Tbsp. unsalted butter
- 1 Tbsp. vegetable oil
- ½ cup low-sodium chicken broth
- 1 cup grated Parmesan

1 Place lemon zest, garlic and parsley on a cutting board. Gather and chop repeatedly until mixture resembles coarse sand. Set aside.

2 Place chicken between 2 sheets of waxed paper and pound flat with a rolling pin. Season with salt and pepper.

3 Melt butter with oil in a large skillet over medium-high heat. Add chicken; cook until browned, 2 to 3 minutes per side. Transfer to a plate and cover loosely with foil to keep warm.

4 Pour off fat from skillet and add broth. Increase heat to high and bring to a boil,

stirring to pick up browned bits. Boil until liquid has thickened and reduced to 2 Tbsp., about 2 minutes.

5 Return chicken to skillet; top with cheese. Reduce heat to medium and cover. Heat until cheese is melted

and chicken is cooked through, 3 minutes. Transfer to plates and drizzle with juices from skillet. Sprinkle with lemon-garlic mixture. **PER SERVING:** 365 Cal., 18g Fat (7g Sat.), 122mg Chol., 0g Fiber, 47g Pro., 1g Carb., 604mg Sod.

SMART TIP

✳ **Plan ahead.** Make the lemon-garlic mixture a day in advance; keep it covered and chilled.

MARK THOMAS; FOOD STYLING: JOYCE SANGIRARDI

SMART TIPS

✻ Add more parts.
You can make this rich dish with chicken drumsticks, or a mix of thighs and drumsticks, if you prefer.

✻ Choose a side.
Sweet potatoes go nicely with this dish, but basmati rice or rice noodles also make good accompaniments.

Chicken Thighs with Spicy Peanut Sauce

Prep: 5 min.
Cook: 40 min.
Serves: 4
Cost per serving:

$1.30

- 4 bone-in, skin-on chicken thighs (about 1 lb. total)
- Salt and pepper
- 2 Tbsp. unsalted butter
- 2 Tbsp. vegetable oil
- 1 onion, chopped
- 1 cup low-sodium chicken broth
- ½ cup creamy peanut butter
- 1 tsp. crushed red pepper
- Juice of 1 lime
- 2 Tbsp. chopped cilantro, optional

1 Trim chicken of excess fat and season on all sides with salt and pepper.

2 Melt butter with oil in a large skillet over medium-high heat. Add chicken and cook, turning often, until lightly browned, about 10 minutes total.

3 Remove chicken to a plate and pour off all but 1 Tbsp. fat from skillet. Add onion and cook, stirring, until softened, 3 to 5 minutes. Add broth and cook, stirring to pick up any browned bits on bottom of skillet. Stir in peanut butter and ¼ cup water. Cook, stirring, until sauce is smooth and creamy. (If sauce appears too thick, add more water, 1 Tbsp. at a time, to reach desired consistency.) Stir in crushed red pepper.

4 Return chicken to skillet; turn to coat with sauce. Cover skillet, reduce heat to medium-low and cook until chicken is cooked through, about 25 minutes. Remove chicken to serving platter. Skim off any excess fat from sauce, stir in lime juice and 1 Tbsp. cilantro, if using, and spoon sauce over chicken. Sprinkle with remaining cilantro, if desired, and serve.

PER SERVING: 519 Cal., 43g Fat (12g Sat), 94mg Chol., 2g Fiber, 25g Pro., 10g Carb., 505mg Sod.

RYAN BENYI, FOOD STYLING: ANDREA STEINBERG

Easy Broiled Drumsticks

Prep: 15 min.
Cook: 30 min.
Serves: 4
Cost per serving:

86¢

- 8 chicken drumsticks
- 2 Tbsp. unsalted butter
- 1 clove garlic, chopped
- 2 Tbsp. lemon juice
- Salt and pepper

1 Position oven rack about 8 inches from heat source. Preheat broiler; line a broiling pan with foil. Pat drumsticks dry and trim off fat. Arrange chicken in a single layer on prepared pan.

2 Melt butter with garlic and lemon juice over medium-low heat. Season drumsticks with salt and pepper. Brush each lightly with lemon butter.

3 Broil, turning often and brushing with lemon butter, until chicken is browned and crisp and has no traces of pink juices when pierced, about 30 minutes. Cool slightly. Serve with barbecue sauce, honey mustard or any other sauce for dipping, if desired.

PER SERVING: 279 Cal., 17g Fat (7g Sat.), 110mg Chol., 0g Fiber, 28g Pro., 1g Carb., 95mg Sod.

CHARLES SCHILLER, FOOD STYLING: A.J. BATTIFARANO

Slow-Cooker Barbecue Turkey Meatballs

✳ SMART TIPS

✳ **Chill out.** The turkey mixture is sticky. If you're having trouble forming it into meatballs, try covering it and refrigerating for 30 minutes.

✳ **Fire it up.** You can use a spicy barbecue sauce to give this recipe a kick.

✳ **Swap meats.** This crowd-pleasing recipe also may be made with ground chicken or lean ground beef, if you prefer.

Prep: 15 min.
Cook: 4 hr.
Serves: 6
Cost per serving:

$1.20

- 2 Tbsp. vegetable oil
- 1 small onion, grated
- 1 stalk celery, chopped
- 1 clove garlic, minced

- 1 lb. ground turkey breast
- 1 large egg, lightly beaten
- ½ cup rolled oats (do not use instant)
- 2 cups barbecue sauce

1 Warm vegetable oil in a small skillet over medium-high heat. Add onion and celery and cook, stirring, until softened, about 4 minutes. Add garlic and sauté 1 minute longer. Transfer to a small bowl and let cool.

2 Place turkey in a large bowl. Add onion mixture, egg and oats. Use your fingers to gently but thoroughly blend ingredients (do not overmix). Dampen hands lightly and form mixture into about 20 1½-inch meatballs.

3 Pour a small amount of sauce over bottom of slow cooker. Add meatballs, alternating with sauce. Pour in ½ cup water. Cover and cook on high until meatballs are cooked through, 3½ to 4 hours.

PER SERVING: 275 Cal., 16g Fat (3g Sat.), 95mg Chol., 2g Fiber, 17g Pro., 17g Carb., 790mg Sod.

RYAN BENYI; FOOD STYLING: ANDREA STEINBERG

Lemon-Rosemary Chicken

Prep: 10 min.
Cook: 4½ hr.
Serves: 4
Cost per serving:
$1.96

- **1 4-lb. whole chicken, rinsed and patted dry**
- **1 lemon**
- **3 sprigs fresh rosemary**
- **2 cloves garlic**
- **3 Tbsp. unsalted butter**
- **Salt and pepper**

1 Rinse chicken inside and out with lukewarm water; pat dry. Halve lemon and place inside cavity along with rosemary and garlic. Fold wings under and tie legs together. Rub chicken with 2 Tbsp. butter and sprinkle with salt and pepper.

2 Place chicken, breast side up, on a small rack inside slow cooker. Cover and cook on high until an instant-read thermometer inserted into thigh registers 180°F, 4 to 4½ hours.

3 Preheat broiler to high. Melt remaining 1 Tbsp. butter. Transfer chicken, breast side up, to a foil-lined baking sheet. Brush chicken with melted butter and broil to brown skin, 2 to 3 minutes. Let chicken rest for 10 minutes on a cutting board before carving and serving.
PER SERVING: 332 Cal., 12g Fat (6g Sat.), 154mg Chol., 0g Fiber, 53g Pro., 1g Carb., 440mg Sod.

SMART TIP

✳ **Be cost-savvy.** A whole chicken works well in this simple recipe, and it costs less than precut pieces. If you prefer the convenience of chicken parts, try leg quarters, which are easy to handle and less expensive than breasts.

Spicy Chicken Stew

Prep: 15 min.
Cook: 4 hr.
Serves: 6
Cost per serving:
$2.22

- **2 baking potatoes (about 1½ lb.), peeled and cut into chunks (3⅓ cups)**
- **1 10-oz. package frozen sweet corn**
- **2 stalks celery, chopped**
- **2 carrots, peeled and cut into chunks (about 1 cup)**
- **1 onion, thickly sliced**
- **2 cloves garlic, minced**
- **1 12.5-oz. jar salsa**
- **2 tsp. salt**
- **1½ tsp. ground cumin**
- **1 tsp. chili powder**
- **½ tsp. pepper**
- **1 skinless, boneless chicken breast, halved (about 1 lb.)**
- **4 skinless, boneless chicken thighs (about 10.5 oz.)**
- **2½ cups chicken broth**
- **4 6-inch corn tortillas**

1 Place potatoes, corn, celery, carrots, onion and garlic in slow cooker. Stir in salsa, salt, cumin, chili powder and pepper. Distribute chicken pieces evenly on top of vegetables and pour broth over chicken. Cover slow cooker and cook stew on high for 4 hours.

2 Transfer chicken to a plate and shred with two forks into bite-size chunks; return meat to slow cooker. Cut tortillas into strips and stir into stew. Serve warm.
PER SERVING: 355 Cal., 6g Fat (1g Sat.), 85mg Chol., 6g Fiber, 34g Pro., 42g Carb., 1,659mg Sod.

SMART TIP

✳ **Garnish well.** This stew is great topped with cilantro, avocado, lime or tortilla chips.

SMART TIPS

❋ **Turn up the heat.** Seed and chop a jalapeño chili and sprinkle onto each layer to spice up the casserole. Add a few shakes of hot sauce while layering.

❋ **Change cheeses.** Swap shredded Cheddar in place of the Monterey Jack. Alternatively, combine them, or use a Mexican cheese blend.

❋ **Kick up the sauce.** For an even more authentic flavor, spoon in enchilada sauce instead of pasta sauce.

Cheesy Chicken Taco Casserole

Prep: 20 min.
Bake: 30 min.
Serves: 4
Cost per serving:

$2.32

- 1½ lb. skinless, boneless chicken breasts
- Salt and pepper
- 1 24-oz. jar pasta sauce
- 9 5-inch corn tortillas
- 1 cup chopped cilantro
- 2 cups shredded Monterey Jack (8 oz.)
- 1 small tomato, sliced

1 Preheat oven to 400°F. Season chicken with salt and pepper. Place in a small skillet and add cold water to cover. Bring to a simmer over medium-high heat. Reduce heat to medium-low and cook, turning once or twice, until opaque and firm, about 10 minutes. Remove, let cool and cut into small pieces or shred. You should have about 3 cups cut-up chicken.

2 Spread ⅓ of sauce over bottom of a 7-by-11-inch baking dish. Arrange 3 tortillas, slightly overlapping, on top. Arrange ⅓ of chicken and cilantro over tortillas. Top with ⅓ of cheese. Make two more layers of sauce, tortillas, chicken, cilantro and cheese. Arrange tomato on final layer of cheese. Cover with foil; bake until bubbly, about 20 minutes. Remove foil and cook until top is lightly browned, 10 minutes more.

PER SERVING: 316 Cal., 14g Fat (8g Sat.), 105mg Chol., 2g Fiber, 37g Pro., 10g Carb., 1,092mg Sod.

CHARLES SCHILLER, FOOD STYLING: LYNN MILLER

Grilled Chicken Quesadillas

Prep: 10 min.
Cook: 32 min.
Serves: 4
Cost per serving:
$2.31

- 1 15.5-oz. can black beans, drained and rinsed
- 3½ cups shredded, cooked rotisserie chicken, skin removed
- 6 oz. grated Monterey Jack
- ¼ cup sliced pickled jalapeño chilies, chopped
- Salt
- 4 10-inch flour tortillas

1 Preheat oven to 200°F and line a large baking sheet with foil or parchment. Place beans in a large bowl and use a potato masher or fork to mash them slightly. Add chicken, cheese and jalapeños and stir to combine. Season with salt.

2 Place 1 tortilla on a work surface and spread a quarter of chicken mixture over half of tortilla. Fold other half of tortilla over to form a half-moon, pressing firmly. Repeat with remaining chicken mixture and tortillas.

3 Warm a ridged grill pan or a 12-inch skillet over medium heat. Cook 1 quesadilla at a time, turning carefully once, until cheese is melted and tortillas are golden, 2 to 4 minutes per side. Transfer grilled quesadilla to prepared baking sheet and place in oven to keep warm.

Repeat with remaining quesadillas. When all quesadillas are grilled, cut each into 4 wedges and serve immediately. **PER SERVING:** 666 Cal., 29g Fat (13g Sat.), 153mg Chol., 5g Fiber, 54g Pro., 45g Carb., 1,261mg Sod.

SMART TIP

❋ **Add on.** Offer bowls of sour cream, guacamole and salsa on the side.

YUNHEE KIM, FOOD STYLING: LYNN MILLER

Caribbean Jerk Chicken

Prep: 10 min.
Cook: 15 min.
Serves: 4
Cost per serving:

$2.30

- Salt
- 2 tsp. Caribbean jerk seasoning
- 4 6-oz. boneless, skinless chicken breast halves
- ¼ cup canola oil
- 1 jalapeño chili, seeded and finely chopped
- 3 scallions, finely chopped
- ¼ cup fresh lime juice (from 3 limes)
- 1 10-oz. bag shredded slaw mix (any variety)

1 Sprinkle salt and 1 tsp. jerk seasoning all over chicken; set aside. Warm 2 Tbsp. oil in a large nonstick skillet over medium-high heat. Cook chicken until browned on both sides and cooked through, 5 minutes per side.

2 In a large bowl, toss together remaining 1 tsp. jerk seasoning, jalapeño, scallions, lime juice, 2 Tbsp. canola oil and slaw mix. Season mixture lightly with salt. Place vegetable mixture on a large platter and top with cooked chicken breasts. Serve warm or at room temperature.

PER SERVING: 337 Cal., 16g Fat (2g Sat.), 99mg Chol., 2g Fiber, 40g Pro., 7g Carb., 524mg Sod.

Chicken with Herbed Dumplings

SMART TIPS

✳ **Make it a meal.** Toss a salad with plenty of colorful vegetables on the side to round out the dinner.

✳ **Save for later.** This comforting dish freezes well. Make extras and freeze in single-serving containers for last-minute meals.

✳ **Take a shortcut.** Use a rotisserie chicken instead of cooking your own.

BEEF & LAMB

PORK

FISH

VEGETABLES

Prep: 30 min.
Cook: 4½ hr.
Serves: 4
Cost per serving:

$1.96

CHICKEN:
- 1 whole chicken (3½ to 4 lb.)
- 2 carrots, cut into 2-inch pieces
- 1 celery rib, cut into 2-inch pieces
- 1 onion, quartered
- 1 bay leaf
- 4 Tbsp. unsalted butter
- 4 Tbsp. all-purpose flour
- Salt and pepper

DUMPLINGS:
- 1½ cups all-purpose flour
- 1 Tbsp. baking powder
- ½ tsp. salt
- 2 Tbsp. chopped fresh herbs, such as thyme and oregano
- 2 Tbsp. unsalted butter
- 1 large egg
- ½ cup milk

1 Make chicken: Put first five ingredients in slow cooker. Pour in 6 cups cold water. Cover and cook on high until chicken is tender, about 3½ hours. Remove chicken from cooker and set aside. When cool, remove meat and shred into large pieces.

2 Strain cooking liquid and set aside. Melt butter in a saucepan over medium-high heat. Add flour and whisk until smooth. Add cooking liquid to pan, increase heat to high, bring to a boil and whisk until smooth and slightly thickened. Return sauce and chicken to slow cooker. Season with salt and pepper.

3 Make dumplings: In a small bowl, combine flour, baking powder, salt and herbs. Add butter and use fingertips or a pastry cutter to work butter into dry ingredients until mixture resembles coarse crumbs. Whisk egg and milk to blend, then stir into flour mixture to form a sticky batter. Drop batter by tablespoon into cooker. Cover and cook on high until dumplings are fluffy, about 1 hour.

PER SERVING: 514 Cal., 22g Fat (12g Sat.), 152mg Chol., 3g Fiber, 28g Pro., 51g Carb., 910mg Sod.

Ricotta-and-Ham-Stuffed Chicken Breasts

Prep: 10 min.
Cook: 10 min.
Serves: 4
Cost per serving:

$1.68

- ½ cup ricotta
- ¼ cup grated Parmesan
- ⅓ cup finely chopped fresh basil leaves
- 1 clove garlic, minced
- 4 boneless, skinless chicken breast halves (about 5 oz. each)
- 4 thin slices deli ham
- Salt and pepper
- ¼ cup all-purpose flour
- 1 Tbsp. olive oil
- 1 Tbsp. unsalted butter

1 In a small bowl, combine ricotta, Parmesan, basil and garlic. Set aside.

2 Rinse chicken and pat dry. Cut a slit along thick edge of each breast half, forming a pocket. Open breast halves like a book and lay one slice of ham in each.

3 Spoon ¼ of ricotta mixture on top of each ham slice, then close chicken over filling and fasten with toothpicks.

4 Season chicken with salt and pepper. Dredge chicken on both sides with flour until well coated. Discard remaining flour.

5 In a large skillet, warm oil and butter over medium-high heat until butter melts and begins to foam. Add chicken to pan and cook 5 minutes; flip and cook on second side for an additional 4 to 5 minutes, until chicken has no traces of pink juices when pierced. Serve hot.

PER SERVING: 363 Cal., 17g Fat (7g Sat.), 125mg Chol., 0g Fiber, 44g Pro., 9g Carb., 821mg Sod.

✳ SMART TIPS

✳ **Fill the plate.** Pasta tossed with butter or olive oil, shaved Parmesan and salt and pepper makes a great side dish. Offer a green vegetable (we chose steamed broccoli) or a salad to round out the meal.

✳ **Swap spices.** If fresh basil is out of season, substitute 1½ Tbsp. dried basil instead.

PREP BREASTS FOR COOKING

Take a few minutes to pound breasts to a uniform thickness to make for quick, even cooking—great for busy weeknights.

1 **Get ready.** Rinse uncooked chicken breasts and pat dry. Place each chicken breast individually on a sheet of waxed paper on a firm countertop.

2 **Start pounding.** Place another sheet of waxed paper on top. Using a rolling pin or the flat side of a meat mallet, and working outward from the center of the chicken, lightly pound each breast.

3 **Keep them even.** Pound the chicken breasts to a uniform thickness. When you're done with one breast, move on to another, making sure all are of equal thickness. Refrigerate chicken until ready to cook.

CHICKEN & TURKEY

BEEF & LAMB

PORK

FISH

VEGETABLES

Teriyaki Chicken Drumsticks

Prep: 5 min.
Cook: 30 min.
Serves: 4
Cost per serving:

$1.01

- ½ cup low-sodium soy sauce
- 2 Tbsp. packed dark brown sugar
- 1 clove garlic, chopped
- ½-inch piece fresh ginger, peeled and chopped
- 1½ tsp. cornstarch
- 8 chicken drumsticks (about 2 lb.)
- Salt and pepper

1 Combine soy sauce, brown sugar, garlic, ginger and cornstarch in a small saucepan. Add 2 Tbsp. water and bring to a boil over high heat, stirring constantly until thickened, about 2 minutes. Cool slightly and strain, discarding solids. Preheat broiler to high and place a broiling rack 6 to 8 inches from heat source. (Alternatively, light a charcoal fire and let coals burn to a gray ash.)

2 Arrange drumsticks snugly on a large foil-lined rimmed baking sheet and season with salt and pepper on all sides. Pour over sauce and turn drumsticks several times to coat thoroughly. Broil or grill until chicken is browned, 25 to 30 minutes, or until juices run clear when chicken is pierced with a knife. While cooking, turn pan around from back to front every 2 to 3 minutes and use tongs to turn drumsticks over.

If liquid in baking sheet starts to scorch, add water, ¼ cup at a time.

3 Remove drumsticks from pan and cool slightly before serving.
PER SERVING: 197 Cal., 4g Fat (1g Sat.), 96mg Chol., 0g Fiber, 28g Pro., 11g Carb., 1,175mg Sod.

SMART TIP

✳ **Remove the solids.** Be sure to strain the sauce—the garlic and ginger will burn if left in.

CHARLES SCHILLER; FOOD STYLING: STEPHANA BOTTOM

SMART TIPS

✳ **Try a different pan.** Instead of using a skillet, cook the sandwiches on a griddle or, if you have one, a panini press.

✳ **Swap the bread.** If you don't care for rye bread, make the sandwiches on whole-wheat bread or pumpernickel instead.

Turkey Reubens

Prep: 10 min.
Cook: 20 min.
Serves: 4
Cost per serving:

$2.26

- ¼ cup low-fat mayonnaise
- 1½ tsp. ketchup
- 3 Tbsp. unsalted butter, softened
- 8 slices rye bread
- 1 cup sauerkraut, well drained
- ¾ lb. sliced deli turkey breast
- 4 oz. Swiss cheese, thinly sliced

1 Combine mayonnaise and ketchup in a small bowl and whisk to combine. Butter each slice of bread evenly on one side. Place bread buttered side down on work surface and spread with mayonnaise mixture, then pile sauerkraut on top. Arrange turkey slices on top of sauerkraut, then place cheese on turkey. Top with remaining bread slices, placing buttered sides up.

2 Warm large skillet over medium-low heat. Place sandwiches in skillet and grill until bread is brown and crisp, 5 to 8 minutes. Using a spatula, carefully turn sandwiches and continue to grill until second side is brown and crisp, another 5 to 7 minutes, pressing down once or twice with spatula to flatten. If all sandwiches won't fit in skillet together, grill two at a time. Place finished sandwiches on a platter and tent with foil to keep warm while cooking remaining sandwiches.

PER SERVING: 505 Cal., 21g Fat (11g Sat.), 123mg Chol., 6g Fiber, 39g Pro., 38g Carb., 1,067mg Sod.

FRANCES JANISCH; FOOD STYLING: LYNN MILLER

White Bean and Chicken Chili

Prep: 30 min.
Cook: 6 hr.
Serves: 6
Cost per serving:
$1.97

- 1 Tbsp. vegetable oil
- 2 whole bone-in chicken breasts (about 3 lb.)
- Salt and pepper
- 2 onions, chopped
- 4 cloves garlic, chopped
- 2 4-oz. cans roasted green chilies, drained
- 1 Tbsp. ground cumin
- 2 15-oz. cans white beans, rinsed and drained
- 4 cups low-sodium chicken broth

1 Warm oil in a skillet over medium-high heat. Sprinkle chicken with salt and pepper; place skin side down in skillet; cook until brown, turning once, about 6 minutes total. Transfer to a plate; remove skin. Drain all but 2 Tbsp. fat from skillet. Add onions and garlic; sauté until softened, 5 minutes. Stir onion mixture, chilies, 1 cup water, cumin, chicken, beans and broth into slow cooker.

2 Cover and cook on low for 6 hours, stirring twice. Remove 1 cup beans plus ½ cup liquid from slow cooker. Puree in a blender; return to slow cooker. Shred chicken and return to slow cooker. Serve hot.

PER SERVING: 296 Cal., 3g Fat (0g Sat.), 0mg Chol., 15g Fiber, 17g Pro., 52g Carb., 410mg Sod.

CHARLES SCHILLER; FOOD STYLING: TARA BENCH

Turkey Cutlets with Fresh Corn

CHARLES SCHILLER; FOOD STYLING: LYNN MILLER

SMART TIPS

✳ Swap meat. You can make this recipe with chicken cutlets instead of turkey, if you prefer, or with boneless pork chops. Alternatively, try this summery dish with a mild white fish, such as tilapia, or with shrimp.

✳ Enjoy anytime. If you crave this dish when fresh corn is out of season, use frozen kernels instead. Thaw just before using.

Prep: 10 min.
Cook: 10 min.
Serves: 4
Cost per serving:

$2.49

- 4 turkey cutlets, patted dry (1 lb.)
- Salt and pepper
- 1½ Tbsp. unsalted butter
- 1 Tbsp. olive oil
- 1 shallot, finely chopped
- ½ red bell pepper, seeded and diced
- ½ cup low-sodium chicken broth
- 1 cup fresh corn kernels (from 2 small ears of corn)
- 1 Tbsp. Dijon mustard
- 1 Tbsp. chopped fresh parsley, optional

1 Sprinkle cutlets with salt and pepper. Warm butter and oil in a large skillet over medium-high heat until butter is foaming. Cook cutlets until browned, turning once, 3 to 4 minutes. Transfer to a plate and cover loosely with foil to keep warm.

2 Add shallot and bell pepper to pan and cook, stirring frequently, until softened, about 3 minutes. Pour in chicken broth and bring to a boil, scraping browned bits off bottom of pan with a wooden spoon. Add corn and mustard and continue to boil, stirring frequently, until sauce thickens a bit, 2 to 3 minutes more. Place cutlets in skillet and turn to coat with sauce. Add any accumulated juices from turkey plate to skillet, as well as parsley, if desired; stir. Serve turkey with sauce immediately.

PER SERVING: 249 Cal., 11g Fat (4g Sat.), 94mg Chol., 2g Fiber, 28g Pro., 11g Carb., 311mg Sod.

Chicken Salad Club Sandwiches

Prep: 30 min.
Serves: 8
Cost per serving:

$1.93

- 1 fully cooked rotisserie chicken (about 3 lb.)
- 2 Tbsp. lemon juice
- 1 cup reduced-fat mayonnaise
- Salt and pepper
- 24 slices sandwich bread, toasted

- 16 thin tomato slices (from 2 large tomatoes)
- 16 length-cut dill pickle slices, drained and patted dry
- 8 large green-leaf lettuce leaves (from 1 large head)

1 Remove meat from chicken and cut into large chunks. Mix chicken with lemon juice and ¼ cup mayonnaise in a large bowl. Season with salt and pepper.

2 Making 1 sandwich at a time, spread 3 slices of toast with mayonnaise. Top 1 slice with ½ cup chicken salad; season with salt and pepper. Top with second piece of toast, mayonnaise side up. Add 2 slices of tomato, 2 slices of pickle and a lettuce leaf. Top with a third piece of toast, mayonnaise side down.

3 Lightly press sandwich down and cut in half diagonally. Secure with toothpicks. Repeat with remaining ingredients.

PER SERVING: 492 Cal., 18g Fat (3g Sat.), 107mg Chol., 2g Fiber, 42g Pro., 40g Carb., 994mg Sod.

SMART TIPS

✳ **Add some spice.** Stir ½ cup of jarred chutney and a dash of curry powder into the chicken mixture.

✳ **Pile on.** Add sliced onion or bacon to these sandwiches.

Chicken Piccata

Prep: 10 min.
Cook: 20 min.
Serves: 4
Cost per serving:

91¢

- 2 whole boneless, skinless chicken breasts (about 1½ lb.), cut in half
- Salt and pepper
- ¼ cup all-purpose flour
- 3 Tbsp. unsalted butter
- 2 Tbsp. vegetable oil
- ¼ cup lemon juice
- ¾ cup low-sodium chicken broth
- ¼ cup chopped fresh parsley

1 Place chicken between 2 sheets of waxed paper and pound until thin. Sprinkle chicken with salt and pepper and dredge in flour.

2 Warm 1 Tbsp. butter and 1 Tbsp. vegetable oil in a large skillet over medium-high heat until butter foams. Add 2 chicken breast halves and cook without moving until browned, 3 minutes. Turn and cook until firm and browned on both sides, 3 minutes more. Transfer to a plate and cover loosely with foil to keep warm.

3 Add 1 Tbsp. butter and remaining 1 Tbsp. oil to skillet; cook remaining chicken breast halves. Transfer to plate and cover to keep warm.

4 Add lemon juice and broth to skillet and bring to a boil, scraping up any browned bits from bottom of pan with a wooden spoon. Boil, stirring occasionally, until thickened, about 5 minutes. Remove from heat, add remaining 1 Tbsp. butter and parsley and stir until butter melts. Season with salt and pepper. Pour sauce over chicken and serve immediately.

PER SERVING: 368 Cal., 19g Fat (7g Sat.), 123mg Chol., 1g Fiber, 41g Pro., 8g Carb., 418mg Sod.

Lemon-Herb Chicken Thighs

SMART TIPS

✳ Make it a meal. Serve the chicken thighs with white rice and steamed broccoli or spinach for a weeknight supper.

✳ Switch it up. Try this dish with another herb, such as thyme or sage, or with orange juice in place of lemon.

✳ Save it for a sandwich. Keep any leftover chicken for lunch. Simply remove meat from bones, shred it by hand and serve it with your favorite sandwich toppings on a roll or French bread.

Prep: 10 min.
Cook: 24 min.
Serves: 6
Cost per serving:

73¢

- 6 bone-in, skin-on chicken thighs (about 1½ lb.), excess fat trimmed
- 3 Tbsp. lemon juice
- 2 Tbsp. olive oil
- 1 Tbsp. minced fresh rosemary or 2 tsp. dried
- 1 clove garlic, minced
- Salt and pepper

1 Preheat broiler. Rinse chicken thighs; pat dry. Arrange thighs, skin side down, on a broiler pan. In a small bowl, combine lemon juice, olive oil, rosemary and garlic. Brush ⅓ of mixture over chicken and sprinkle with salt and pepper. Broil 4 to 6 inches from heat until lightly browned, about 7 minutes.

2 Using tongs, turn chicken thighs skin side up. Brush ⅓ of lemon-juice mixture over skin and sprinkle with salt and pepper. Broil until thighs are browned, about 7 minutes.

3 Turn off broiler and set oven to 450°F. Brush final ⅓ of lemon-juice mixture over chicken (discard any that's left over) and return pan to oven. Bake until juices run clear when pricked with a fork and meat is no longer pink at the bone, 10 minutes. Serve hot.
PER SERVING: 243 Cal., 19g Fat (5g Sat.), 79mg Chol., 0g Fiber, 16g Pro., 1g Carb., 266mg Sod.

CHARLES SCHILLER, FOOD STYLING: LYNN MILLER

Braised Chicken with Potatoes

Prep: 25 min.
Cook: 2 hr. 15 min.
Serves: 4
Cost per serving:

$2.08

- ½ lb. boneless, skinless chicken thighs, fat trimmed
- Salt and pepper
- ¼ cup all-purpose flour
- 2 Tbsp. olive oil
- ½ cup white wine
- 1½ cups low-sodium chicken broth
- 1 lb. Yukon gold potatoes, peeled and cut into 1½-inch cubes
- 1 8-oz. package frozen artichoke hearts
- 2 cloves garlic, crushed
- 1 lemon

1 Rinse chicken and pat dry; season with salt and pepper. Spread flour in a shallow bowl and dredge each piece of chicken on both sides. In a large pan over medium-high heat, warm olive oil. Add chicken and sauté, turning once, until golden brown on both sides, about 8 minutes. Remove chicken from pan and transfer to slow cooker.

2 Reduce heat on stove to medium and add wine to pan (it will steam vigorously). With a wooden spoon, scrape up any browned bits that cling to pan. Bring to a boil, then pour liquid into slow cooker.

3 Add broth, potatoes, artichoke hearts and garlic to slow cooker. Peel two 3-inch strips of lemon peel and add to slow cooker, along with juice from lemon.

4 Turn slow cooker to high. Cover and cook until chicken and potatoes are cooked through and tender, 2 hours and 15 minutes. Serve hot.

PER SERVING: 284 Cal., 15g Fat (2g Sat.), 49mg Chol., 5g Fiber, 17g Pro., 18g Carb., 402mg Sod.

CHARLES SCHILLER, FOOD STYLING: LYNN MILLER

BEEF & LAMB

PORK

FISH

VEGETABLES

Corn Flake–Crusted Chicken

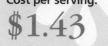

Prep: 10 min.
Cook: 30 min.
Serves: 4
Cost per serving:

$1.43

- 4 boneless, skinless chicken breast halves
- ½ cup all-purpose flour
- 1 tsp. dried thyme
- 1 tsp. cayenne pepper
- Salt and pepper
- 2 large eggs
- 6 cups coarsely crushed corn flakes
- 3 Tbsp. unsalted butter, melted

1 Preheat oven to 375°F. Line a rimmed baking sheet with foil; mist with cooking spray. Place each chicken breast half between two sheets of waxed paper. With a rolling pin or meat mallet, pound chicken to an even ½-inch thickness. In a shallow dish, combine flour, thyme, cayenne pepper, salt and pepper; mix with a fork. In a second shallow dish, whisk eggs to combine. Spread corn-flake crumbs on a second rimmed baking sheet.

2 Dredge chicken in seasoned flour, turning to coat, then dip in egg mixture. Remove chicken, allowing excess egg to drip off, then press both sides firmly into corn-flake crumbs. Transfer chicken to lined baking sheet. Discard any remaining flour, egg and corn flakes.

3 Drizzle chicken evenly with melted butter. Bake until coating is crisp and chicken is cooked through, about 30 minutes. Serve immediately.

PER SERVING: 391 Cal., 12g Fat (4g Sat.), 157mg Chol., 2g Fiber, 33g Pro., 37g Carb., 730mg Sod.

SMART TIP

✳ **Turn up the heat.** For a spicier kick, add some chili powder to the seasoned flour.

BEEF & LAMB

PORK

FISH

VEGETABLES

SMART TIPS

☀ Save leftovers. Meatballs freeze well. Divide the leftovers into single-serving containers and freeze (don't forget to label the containers, including the date).

☀ Serve it well. Try these meatballs over pasta or rice, or spoon them into whole-grain buns for sandwiches. A green salad rounds out the meal.

☀ Try flavored sausage. If you like your meatballs with a little bite, use hot Italian sausage. If you prefer them on the milder side, use plain or sweet sausage (the flavor isn't really sweet, just less hot).

Turkey Meatballs

Prep: 20 min.
Cook: 5 hr.
Serves: 8
Cost per serving:

$1.77

- 1 Tbsp. extra-virgin olive oil
- 4 cloves garlic, finely chopped
- Salt

- 2 28-oz. cans crushed tomatoes
- ½ tsp. dried oregano
- 1¼ lb. lean ground turkey
- 2 lb. turkey sausage, casings removed, crumbled
- 1¼ cups plain dry bread crumbs
- ¾ cup grated Parmesan
- 2 large eggs
- ¼ cup finely chopped fresh parsley

1 Warm olive oil in medium skillet over medium heat. Add half of garlic and cook, stirring, until fragrant, about 30 seconds. Scrape into slow cooker. Add ¾ tsp. salt, tomatoes, and oregano; stir to combine.

2 In a large mixing bowl, combine turkey, sausage, bread crumbs, cheese, eggs, parsley, remaining garlic and 1 tsp. salt. Use your fingers to blend all ingredients together; do not overmix. Form mixture into 2-inch balls and place in slow cooker. Spoon tomato mixture over meatballs to cover.

3 Cover and cook on low until meatballs are cooked through, 4 to 5 hours.

PER SERVING: 397 Cal., 18g Fat (6g Sat.), 151mg Chol., 5g Fiber, 32g Pro., 29g Carb., 1,578mg Sod.

Grilled Chicken, Peach and Arugula Salad

Prep: 5 min.
Cook: 12 min.
Serves: 6
Cost per serving:

$1.92

- 5 Tbsp. olive oil
- 1 Tbsp. balsamic vinegar
- 1 Tbsp. finely chopped shallot
- 1 tsp. Dijon mustard
- Salt
- 4 peaches, halved, pits removed
- 4 skinless, boneless chicken breast halves (about 4 oz. each)
- 8 cups baby arugula or other tender salad greens

1 Preheat grill to medium-high (or place a grill pan on stove over medium-high heat).

In a large bowl, whisk together 4 Tbsp. oil, vinegar, shallot, mustard and ½ tsp. salt.

2 Brush peaches with 1 tsp. oil. Grill, cut side down, until peaches are warmed through, about 4 minutes. Remove fruit from grill.

3 Brush chicken on both sides with remaining 2 tsp. oil and sprinkle with salt. Grill until cooked through, turning once, about 8 minutes total. Cut chicken into thin diagonal slices. Cut peaches into ½-inch-thick slices.

4 Add greens to bowl with dressing and toss. Divide greens among serving plates, top with peaches and sliced chicken, and serve.

PER SERVING: 218 Cal., 13g Fat (2g Sat.), 44mg Chol., 1g Fiber, 19g Pro., 8g Carb., 271mg Sod.

Chicken Sausages with Beans

Prep: 10 min.
Cook: 4 hr. 8 min.
Serves: 6
Cost per serving:

$1.86

- 12 oz. chicken sausage with Mediterranean seasonings, cut into ¼-inch rounds
- 1 15-oz. can cannellini beans, drained and rinsed
- 1 15-oz. can garbanzo beans, drained and rinsed
- 1 28-oz. can whole tomatoes, drained and chopped
- 1½ cups low-sodium chicken broth
- 1 bay leaf
- 1 tsp. dried thyme
- ¼ tsp. crushed red pepper
- 1 small head escarole, chopped
- 2 Tbsp. chopped fresh parsley
- ¼ cup coarsely grated Parmesan
- Salt and pepper

1 Combine sausage, beans, tomatoes, broth, bay leaf, thyme and red pepper in slow cooker. Cover and cook on low for 4 hours.

2 Stir in escarole; cook 5 to 8 minutes, until just wilted. Stir in parsley and Parmesan. Season with salt and pepper.

PER SERVING: 285 Cal., 10g Fat (3g Sat.), 47mg Chol., 10g Fiber, 20g Pro., 30g Carb., 1,413mg Sod.

FRANCES JANISCH; FOOD STYLING: LYNN MILLER

CHICKEN & TURKEY

BEEF & LAMB

PORK

FISH

VEGETABLES

Turkey Nachos

Prep: 5 min.
Cook: 23 min.
Serves: 6
Cost per serving:

$1.80

- 2 tsp. vegetable oil
- 1 onion, finely chopped
- 1 clove garlic, chopped
- 1 Tbsp. chili powder
- ½ tsp. ground cumin
- Salt
- 8 oz. lean ground turkey
- 1 9-oz. bag baked corn tortilla chips
- 1 cup canned black beans, rinsed and drained
- 1 cup cherry tomatoes, chopped
- 8 oz. reduced-fat pepper Jack, shredded

1 Preheat oven to 400°F. Warm oil in a skillet over medium heat. Sauté onion until softened, 5 minutes. Add garlic, chili powder, cumin and a pinch of salt; sauté 30 seconds. Add turkey and cook, stirring, 7 minutes.

2 Spread ½ bag of chips in a 9-by-13-inch baking dish. Spoon ½ of turkey mixture over. Spread ½ of beans and ½ of tomatoes over. Sprinkle with ½ of cheese. Repeat with remaining ingredients. Bake uncovered until cheese has melted, 7 to 10 minutes. Serve hot.

PER SERVING: 421 Cal., 20g Fat (8g Sat.), 67mg Chol., 6g Fiber, 22g Pro., 44g Carb., 865mg Sod.

Pasta with Chicken and Artichokes

CHICKEN & TURKEY

BEEF & LAMB

PORK

FISH

VEGETABLES

SMART TIPS

❋ **Use your leftovers.** If you have extra cooked chicken, remove the skin and bones, chop it and use it in this dish instead of buying a rotisserie chicken.

❋ **Make it vegetarian.** Instead of chicken, toss in a can of white beans (drained and rinsed) and swap in vegetable broth.

❋ **Up the nutrients.** Use whole-wheat pasta to add more fiber to this dish. If your family prefers regular pasta, try a whole-wheat blend.

Prep: 15 min.
Cook: 12 min.
Serves: 6
Cost per serving:

$2.20

- 1 lb. penne or ziti
- Salt
- 3 Tbsp. extra-virgin olive oil
- 2 cloves garlic, finely chopped
- ¼ cup kalamata or other black olives, pitted and chopped
- 1 14-oz. can artichoke hearts (about 8), rinsed, drained and chopped
- 2 cups (10 oz.) shredded chicken from 1 rotisserie chicken
- ½ cup low-sodium chicken broth
- 2 Tbsp. finely chopped fresh basil
- ½ cup grated Parmesan

1 Bring a large pot of water to a boil over high heat. Add pasta and 1 Tbsp. salt and cook until tender.

2 While pasta is cooking, warm oil over medium heat in a large skillet. Add garlic; cook until fragrant, stirring, about 30 seconds. Stir in olives, artichoke hearts, chicken, broth and ½ tsp. salt and heat through.

3 Drain pasta. Return to pot and stir in chicken mixture and basil. Adjust seasonings, sprinkle with Parmesan and serve.

PER SERVING: 465 Cal., 14g Fat (3g Sat.), 46mg Chol., 9g Fiber, 31g Pro., 52g Carb., 600mg Sod.

CHARLES SCHILLER; FOOD STYLING: STEPHANA BOTTOM

CHICKEN &
TURKEY

BEEF &
LAMB

PORK

FISH

VEGETABLES

SMART TIPS

✳ Hold the meat.
To make these hearty burritos vegetarian, substitute 1 to 2 cans of drained and rinsed black beans or pinto beans for the chicken, or swap in canned vegetarian refried beans. Garnish with chopped cilantro, pickled jalapeños or sour cream.

✳ Take a side. Serve these burritos with baked tortilla chips and extra salsa, or some ready-made guacamole. A green salad also makes a good accompaniment. Toss it with a quick dressing: Whisk ½ cup buttermilk, ½ cup plain yogurt, 3 Tbsp. white wine vinegar and 1 tsp. honey; season with salt and pepper.

Chicken Burritos

Prep: 20 min.
Cook: 5 min.
Serves: 6
Cost per serving:

$2.00

- 1 Tbsp. vegetable oil
- 1 onion, finely chopped
- 1 clove garlic, finely chopped
- 3 cups shredded skinless cooked chicken, from a rotisserie chicken
- Salt
- 6 flour tortillas
- 3 cups shredded iceberg lettuce
- ¾ cup tomato salsa
- 1½ cups shredded Cheddar

1 Warm vegetable oil in a large skillet over medium-high heat. Add chopped onion and sauté until softened, about 3 minutes. Add garlic and cook, stirring, 1 minute. Stir in chicken and ¼ tsp. salt and cook until heated through, 1 to 2 minutes.

2 Place flour tortillas between 2 moistened paper towels and microwave on high for 10 seconds to soften. Spoon some shredded lettuce onto each tortilla. Top each with chicken, salsa and shredded Cheddar. Roll up burritos, cut in half and serve.
PER SERVING: 492 Cal., 19g Fat (7g Sat.), 90mg Chol., 4g Fiber, 36g Pro., 43g Carb., 1,144mg Sod.

Chicken Breasts with Peppers

Prep: 10 min.
Cook: 16 min.
Serves: 4
Cost per serving:

$1.56

- 4 6-oz. boneless, skinless chicken breast halves
- Salt
- ½ cup all-purpose flour
- 3 Tbsp. vegetable oil
- 2 cloves garlic, chopped
- 1 7-oz. jar roasted red peppers, drained and cut into strips
- ¾ cup low-sodium chicken broth
- 2 Tbsp. red wine vinegar
- 1½ tsp. sugar
- 1 Tbsp. unsalted butter
- 2 Tbsp. chopped fresh parsley

1 Place each chicken breast half between 2 sheets of waxed paper and pound to an even ½-inch thickness. Sprinkle with salt. Coat chicken on both sides with flour; shake off excess.

2 Warm 2 Tbsp. oil in a large skillet over medium-high heat. Cook chicken until golden on both sides and cooked through, 8 to 10 minutes total. Transfer to a plate; cover.

3 Heat remaining oil in skillet. Sauté garlic until fragrant, about 30 seconds. Add peppers and sauté for 1 minute. Add broth, vinegar and sugar; bring to a boil, scraping up browned bits from pan. Reduce heat; simmer until slightly thickened, about 4 minutes. Remove pan from heat; stir in butter and parsley until butter melts. Pour sauce over chicken and serve.

PER SERVING: 385 Cal., 16g Fat (3g Sat.), 106mg Chol., 2g Fiber, 42g Pro., 17g Carb., 541mg Sod.

SMART TIP

❋ **Save money.** Try this recipe with boneless, skinless chicken thighs, which are less expensive.

ALAN RICHARDSON, FOOD STYLING: STEPHANA BOTTOM

BEEF & LAMB

PORK

FISH

VEGETABLES

Coffee-Brined Chicken Drumsticks

Prep: 5 min.
Chill: 2 hr.
Cook: 35 min.
Serves: 4
Cost per serving:

$1.41

- 1½ cups strongly brewed coffee
- ¼ cup salt
- 3 Tbsp. sugar
- 2 Tbsp. chili powder
- ½ tsp. crushed red pepper
- 3 cloves garlic, crushed
- 1 cinnamon stick
- 8 chicken drumsticks (2½ lb. total)

1 In a large bowl, stir together 2 cups water, coffee, salt and sugar until salt and sugar are completely dissolved. Stir in chili powder, red pepper, garlic and cinnamon. Add chicken. Top with a small plate, if needed, to keep chicken submerged. Cover and refrigerate for 2 to 4 hours.

2 Preheat broiler. Lift chicken from brine and place on a broiler pan. (Discard brine.) Broil 4 to 6 inches from heat source until browned, about 10 minutes. Turn chicken pieces and broil until second side is browned, about 10 minutes more.

3 Set oven to 350°F. Move pan to a rack in middle of oven and bake until drumsticks are no longer pink at bone (cut to test), 10 to 15 minutes longer. Serve hot.

PER SERVING: 289 Cal., 13g Fat (4g Sat.), 118mg Chol., 1g Fiber, 29g Pro., 13g Carb., 161mg Sod.

SMART TIPS

✳ **Try other parts.** Drumsticks are fun for kids to eat, but you can make this dish with any chicken parts. It works with turkey, too. You could even brine a whole chicken and roast it for a more elegant presentation.

✳ **Enjoy in warm weather.** This chicken is also delicious grilled. Serve it right away, or chill it and take it on a picnic.

✳ **Keep it plain.** A dark or light coffee roast will work, but be sure to use an unflavored variety for the brine.

KEEP FOOD FRESHER AND TASTIER LONGER

Save money and keep your family safe with simple food-storage tips and tricks.

1 **Store properly.** Before you put food in the fridge or freezer, make sure you use the right-size container. Leaving lots of space between the container lid and your food leads to

faster spoilage and freezer burn. If you're keeping food in a ziplock bag, squeeze out excess air before sealing.

2 **Write it down.** Eating leftovers is a great way to cut costs, but only if you remember to use them. Label containers with the contents and the date, and follow the first-in, first-out rule:

Use up older leftovers before digging into newer ones (but don't keep anything in the fridge for more than four days).

3 **Don't trust your nose.** Although a foul smell is a good indicator of spoilage, not all foods fail the smell test, even after they've turned. Keep track of expiration dates, and look for changes

in color or texture. Food that has a slimy texture or is covered in film should be tossed. If you're not sure, throw it away.

CHICKEN & TURKEY

BEEF & LAMB

PORK

FISH

VEGETABLES

Grilled Turkey, Cheddar and Apple Sandwiches

SMART TIPS

❋ **Choose the right cheese.** Thinly sliced Cheddar from the deli counter or packaged Cheddar slices work best in these sandwiches. Don't use nonfat cheese—it doesn't melt as well.

❋ **Pick your mustard.** Honey mustard is an excellent match for the tart apples, but you can swap in Dijon, if you prefer. You also can make these sandwiches with rye bread.

❋ **Skip the butter.** If you have a panini maker with a nonstick surface, you can press the sandwiches in it until they're golden and crisp—no butter needed.

Prep: 10 min.

Cook: 10 min.

Serves: 4

Cost per serving:

$1.70

- 3 Tbsp. unsalted butter
- 8 slices hearty white or whole-grain bread
- 2 Tbsp. honey mustard
- 4 slices Cheddar
- 16 thin slices deli turkey (about 8 oz.)
- ½ Granny Smith apple, cored and thinly sliced

1 Spread 1½ Tbsp. butter on 1 side of 4 slices of bread, and spread mustard on other side of each slice. Top mustard-covered side of each bread slice with 1 slice Cheddar, followed by ¼ each of turkey and apple slices. Spread remaining butter on 1 side of remaining 4 slices of bread and place them, butter side up, on top of apple slices.

2 Place sandwiches in a large skillet and cook over medium-high heat until golden, about 4 minutes per side. If skillet is too small, cook sandwiches 2 at a time, placing first batch on a plate and covering loosely with foil while cooking second batch. Serve immediately.

PER SERVING: 409 Cal., 18g Fat (9g Sat.), 76mg Chol., 6g Fiber, 29g Pro., 42g Carb., 501mg Sod.

RYAN BENYI, FOOD STYLING: LYNN MILLER

Chicken with Tomatoes and Arugula

Prep: 10 min.
Cook: 20 min.
Serves: 4
Cost per serving:

$2.14

- Four 6-oz. boneless, skinless chicken breast halves, pounded to ½-inch thickness
- Salt
- ½ cup all-purpose flour
- 3 Tbsp. vegetable oil
- ½ onion, finely chopped
- 1 cup low-sodium chicken broth
- 1 15-oz. can chopped tomatoes, drained
- ½ cup pitted, chopped black olives
- 4 cups baby arugula

1 Sprinkle chicken with salt. Place flour in a shallow bowl. Dredge each chicken breast half on both sides with flour, shaking off excess over bowl.

2 Warm 2 Tbsp. oil in a large skillet over medium-high heat. Add chicken and cook until golden on both sides and cooked through, about 10 minutes total. Transfer to a plate; cover with foil to keep warm.

3 Heat remaining 1 Tbsp. oil in skillet. Add onion and cook, stirring, until softened, about 5 minutes. Add broth and tomatoes and cook until sauce has thickened, about 3 minutes. Stir in olives and arugula and cook, stirring, until arugula has wilted, about 1 minute. Season with salt.

4 Pour sauce over chicken and serve.

PER SERVING: 394 Cal., 15g Fat (1g Sat.), 99mg Chol., 1g Fiber, 43g Pro., 20g Carb., 995mg Sod.

CHARLES SCHILLER, FOOD STYLING: ANDREA STEINBERG

SMART TIPS

✻ **Swap the rice.**
If arborio isn't available in your supermarket, try regular short-grain white rice. A medium-grain rice also works, but the dish will have a softer texture.

✻ **Make it a meal.**
A green salad is all you need to make this dish a complete dinner. Pass extra Parmesan on the side.

Risotto with Turkey Sausage

Prep: 5 min.
Cook: 35 min.
Serves: 6
Cost per serving:

$2.20

- **6 cups low-sodium chicken broth**
- **1 Tbsp. olive oil**
- **1 onion, finely chopped**
- **¾ lb. turkey sausage with Italian seasonings, casings removed**
- **2 cups arborio rice**
- **½ cup dry white wine**
- **1 5-oz. package baby spinach (about 6 cups)**
- **¾ cup grated Parmesan**
- **1 Tbsp. unsalted butter**
- **Salt**

1 Bring broth and 2 cups water to a simmer in a medium saucepan. Turn heat to low to keep warm.

2 Warm olive oil in a heavy pot over medium heat. Add onion and cook, stirring, until softened, about 3 minutes. Add sausage and cook, stirring often and breaking up into small pieces, until it loses its pink color, about 5 minutes. Add rice and cook for 1 minute, stirring to coat grains with fat. Add wine and cook until alcohol evaporates, about 2 minutes.

3 Reduce heat to medium-low. Add 2 cups warm broth mixture and simmer, stirring frequently, until rice absorbs liquid. Continue to add liquid, 2 cups at a time, stirring occasionally, until rice is creamy and soft, about 20 minutes (you may not use all of the liquid). Add spinach and stir until wilted, about 2 minutes.

4 Remove pot from heat, stir in cheese and butter and season with salt. Serve immediately.

PER SERVING: 524 Cal., 23g Fat (8g Sat.), 57mg Chol., 2g Fiber, 21g Pro., 53g Carb., 1,198mg Sod.

Stuffed Summer Squash

Prep: 15 min.
Bake: 20 min.
Serves: 4
Cost per serving:

$1.91

- Salt and pepper
- 1 large yellow summer squash (about 8 oz.)
- 1 large zucchini (about 8 oz.)
- 3 Tbsp. olive oil
- 1 onion, chopped
- 1 lb. lean ground turkey
- 1 cup chopped fresh or canned tomatoes
- ½ cup low-sodium chicken broth
- 2 tsp. chopped fresh thyme
- ⅓ cup dry Italian-style bread crumbs
- 2 Tbsp. grated Parmesan

1 Fill a bowl with ice water. Bring a pot of salted water to a boil. Cut squash and zucchini in half lengthwise; place in boiling water. Bring back to a boil; cook until slightly softened, 5 minutes. Transfer both squashes to ice water. Cool for 2 minutes. Remove; pat dry.

2 Scrape out seeds and stringy pulp from each squash half, leaving a large cavity for stuffing. Arrange snugly in a large, lightly oiled ovenproof baking dish.

3 Warm 1 Tbsp. oil in a large skillet over medium-high heat. Add onion and cook, stirring often, until softened, about 3 minutes. Add turkey and cook, stirring to break up until crumbly, 2 to 3 minutes. Stir in tomatoes, broth and thyme. Increase heat to high and cook, stirring often, until turkey is thoroughly cooked and some liquid has evaporated, 5 to 7 minutes. Season with salt and pepper.

4 Preheat oven to 425°F. Place equal amounts of filling in each squash half, piling it high in center. Mix bread crumbs with Parmesan, then sprinkle mixture over squash and drizzle with 2 Tbsp. olive oil. Bake until golden brown on top, about 20 minutes.

PER SERVING: 350 Cal., 21g Fat (5g Sat.), 92mg Chol., 3g Fiber, 25g Pro., 15g Carb., 696mg Sod.

Chicken Thighs with Mustard-Citrus Sauce

Prep: 5 min.
Chill: 1 hr.
Cook: 30 min.
Serves: 8
Cost per serving:

$1.18

- ¼ cup lemon juice
- 1 Tbsp. Worcestershire sauce
- 3 Tbsp. minced garlic
- 3 Tbsp. honey
- 8 skinless, boneless chicken thighs
- 2 Tbsp. olive oil
- Salt and pepper
- 3 Tbsp. chopped shallot
- ¼ tsp. crushed red pepper
- ½ cup orange juice
- ¾ cup low-sodium chicken broth
- ¼ cup Dijon mustard
- ½ tsp. orange zest

1 Mix lemon juice, Worcestershire sauce, 1 Tbsp. garlic and 2 Tbsp. honey in a plastic bag. Add chicken. Marinate in fridge for 1 hour.

2 Warm oil in a large skillet. Remove thighs from marinade, pat dry and sprinkle with salt and pepper. Brown chicken on all sides, about 10 minutes. Remove chicken from pan, add shallots, remaining garlic and crushed red pepper; sauté 2 minutes. Return chicken to pan; add juice and broth. Simmer, turning once, until chicken is cooked through, 10 minutes.

3 Remove chicken to plate. Add mustard, zest and remaining honey to skillet. Bring to a boil and whisk until sauce thickens, about 7 minutes. Spoon over chicken and serve.

PER SERVING: 162 Cal., 6g Fat (1g Sat.), 57mg Chol., 0g Fiber, 14g Pro., 12g Carb., 459mg Sod.

Asian Sesame Noodles with Chicken

Prep: 30 min.
Cook: 20 min.
Serves: 6
Cost per serving:

$1.18

- 1 lb. spaghetti
- Salt and pepper
- 2 boneless, skinless chicken breast halves, trimmed
- ¾ cup creamy or crunchy peanut butter
- 3 Tbsp. reduced-sodium soy sauce
- 3 Tbsp. seasoned rice vinegar
- ½ tsp. crushed red pepper
- 2 Tbsp. sesame oil
- 1 Tbsp. finely chopped fresh ginger
- 1 small cucumber, seeded, sliced and cut crosswise into strips
- 1 plum tomato, sliced
- 2 scallions, thinly sliced

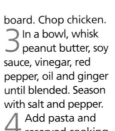

1 Cook pasta in a large pot of boiling salted water, according to package directions, until al dente. Reserve 1 cup cooking water and drain pasta in a colander.

2 Lightly oil a grill pan; place over medium heat. Season chicken with salt and pepper. Grill for 6 to 8 minutes per side, until just cooked through. Transfer to a cutting board. Chop chicken.

3 In a bowl, whisk peanut butter, soy sauce, vinegar, red pepper, oil and ginger until blended. Season with salt and pepper.

4 Add pasta and reserved cooking water to bowl and toss to coat. Add chicken, cucumber and tomato to mixture; toss. Arrange pasta on a serving platter and garnish with scallions.

PER SERVING: 440 Cal., 17g Fat (3g Sat.), 16mg Chol., 3g Fiber, 21g Pro., 51g Carb., 488mg Sod.

RYAN BENYI; FOOD STYLING: STEPHANA BOTTOM

French Bread Pizzas

Prep: 10 min.
Bake: 10 min.
Serves: 4
Cost per serving:
$1.92

- 1 loaf French bread
- 2 Tbsp. olive oil
- 1 clove garlic
- ¾ cup tomato sauce
- 2 cups grated part-skim mozzarella cheese (8 oz.)
- 32 slices turkey pepperoni

1 Preheat oven to 400°F. Slice bread in half lengthwise and then cut each piece in half again to make 4 equal pieces. Brush each piece with ½ Tbsp. olive oil. Place bread on a baking sheet and bake until lightly toasted, 5 minutes.

2 Remove bread from oven and rub cut side of each piece with garlic. Spread tomato sauce over bread, sprinkle with grated cheese and top with turkey pepperoni slices.

3 Place assembled pizzas in oven and bake until cheese is melted and bubbly, 5 to 7 minutes. Cut each piece into thirds and serve immediately.

PER SERVING: 638 Cal., 28g Fat (9g Sat.), 84mg Chol., 3g Fiber, 38g Pro., 60g Carb., 2,152mg Sod.

Cheesy Twice-Baked Potatoes

---

* SMART TIPS

* Try uncured bacon. If your supermarket carries it, buy uncured turkey bacon. It has a richer flavor, is lower in sodium and contains no saturated fat.

* Switch spuds. Try this tasty recipe using sweet potatoes instead of russets, if you prefer.

Prep: 5 min.
Cook: 25 min.
Serves: 4
Cost per serving:

$1.45

- 4 large russet potatoes, scrubbed well
- 6 slices turkey bacon
- 2 Tbsp. unsalted butter
- ½ cup low-fat milk
- Salt and pepper
- 1 cup shredded Cheddar
- 2 scallions, chopped

1 Line a rimmed baking sheet with foil. Preheat broiler, placing oven rack directly beneath heat source. Pierce potatoes all over with a fork and cook on high in microwave until tender, about 20 minutes, turning once. While potatoes are cooking, fry bacon in a small, heavy-bottom skillet over medium-high heat until crisp and brown, about 4 minutes per side. Transfer bacon to paper towels to drain.

When cool enough to handle, crumble bacon and set aside.

2 Put butter and milk in a microwave-safe bowl and microwave until butter has melted, about 2 minutes. With hands covered to protect from heat, cut potatoes in half lengthwise and scoop out flesh with a spoon. Place potato flesh in a medium bowl and break up with a fork; set aside potato skins. Add milk mixture, salt, pepper, ¾ cup cheese and

scallions to bowl with potato flesh and mix well. Stir in bacon. Divide potato mixture among potato skins.

3 Place stuffed potatoes on prepared baking sheet and sprinkle with remaining ¼ cup cheese. Broil potatoes until tops are crisp and bubbling and mixture is heated through, about 4 minutes. Serve hot.

PER SERVING: 323 Cal., 20g Fat (11g Sat.), 65mg Chol., 9g Fiber, 19g Pro., 20g Carb., 635mg Sod.

Beer Can Chicken

Prep: 5 min.
Cook: 1 hr. 15 min.
Serves: 8
Cost per serving:

$2.19

- **2 whole chickens (about 4 lb. each)**
- **1 Tbsp. paprika**
- **1 Tbsp. onion powder**
- **1 Tbsp. garlic powder**
- **1 Tbsp. dried thyme**
- **Salt and pepper**
- **2 12-oz. cans beer**

1 Preheat oven to 350°F. Rinse chickens inside and out; pat dry.

2 Mix paprika, onion powder, garlic powder, thyme, salt and pepper. Rub chickens with spice mixture.

3 Pour about 2 oz. beer out of each can. Set cans upright in a roasting pan large enough to hold both chickens without touching. Set chickens so that cans fit inside cavities, legs facing down. Roast chickens until juices run clear, about 1 hour 15 minutes, basting after 30 minutes.

4 Carefully remove chickens from cans and let rest for 10 to 15 minutes before carving.

PER SERVING: 298 Cal., 20g Fat (5g Sat.), 129mg Chol., 1g Fiber, 29g Pro., 2g Carb., 566mg Sod.

SMART TIP

✳ **Take it outside.** If your grill is large enough, you can make this fun dish outside. Grill over medium heat, covered, for 1 hour 15 minutes to 1 hour 30 minutes. Let it rest for 5 minutes before removing, carving and serving.

Baked Potatoes Stuffed with Turkey, Bacon and Cheddar

Prep: 5 min.
Cook: 22 min.
Serves: 4
Cost per serving:

$1.39

- **4 8-oz. baking potatoes**
- **2 Tbsp. unsalted butter**
- **½ cup milk**
- **¼ tsp. salt**
- **4 oz. grated Cheddar**
- **¼ lb. sliced turkey, chopped**
- **4 slices bacon, cooked crisp and crumbled**
- **2 scallions, white and light green parts, chopped**

1 Preheat oven to 500°F and line a rimmed baking sheet with foil. Pierce potatoes all over with a fork. Arrange on top of paper towels in microwave and cover with damp paper towels. Microwave on high until potatoes are soft when pierced with a skewer, 12 to 14 minutes. Let stand 2 minutes.

2 Split potatoes open lengthwise and scoop flesh into a medium bowl, reserving skins. Stir butter, milk and salt into bowl with potato flesh and mash. Stir in half of cheese and all of turkey, bacon and scallions.

3 Place reserved potato skins on

baking sheet. Stuff potato mixture back into shells, mounding in center if necessary, and sprinkle tops with remaining cheese. Bake until cheese is browned and bubbling and filling is hot, about 8 minutes. Serve immediately.

PER SERVING: 508 Cal., 23g Fat (12g Sat.), 85mg Chol., 5g Fiber, 26g Pro., 51g Carb., 688mg Sod.

BEEF & LAMB

PORK

FISH

VEGETABLES

SMART TIPS

❋ Add some herbs.
Toss some chopped basil or oregano into the tomato sauce and mix gently. Or use bread crumbs with Italian seasonings.

❋ Enjoy a balanced meal. Serve pasta tossed with olive oil and grated Parmesan, and a green veggie, such as broccoli, for a satisfying supper.

❋ Go dark. Boneless, skinless chicken thighs work just as well in this dish.

Skillet Chicken Parmesan

Prep: 10 min.
Cook: 15 min.
Serves: 4
Cost per serving:

$1.90

- **4 boneless, skinless chicken breast halves (about 1 lb.)**
- **¼ cup panko or other plain bread crumbs**
- **¼ cup grated Parmesan**
- **½ tsp. dried basil or 1½ tsp. fresh basil, chopped**
- **Salt and pepper**
- **2 Tbsp. vegetable oil**
- **½ cup all-purpose flour**
- **1 cup tomato sauce**
- **1½ cups grated mozzarella**

1 Place chicken between sheets of waxed paper and pound with a rolling pin or meat mallet to ¼-inch thickness (see page 17).

2 Toast bread crumbs in a dry, ovenproof skillet over medium heat until golden, shaking pan occasionally, 2 to 3 minutes. Transfer to a bowl to cool. Stir in Parmesan and basil.

3 Sprinkle chicken with salt and pepper. Dredge both sides in flour. Warm oil in skillet over medium-high heat. Cook chicken until brown and cooked through, turning once,

about 3 minutes per side.

4 Preheat broiler to high. Remove skillet from heat; spoon tomato sauce over chicken and sprinkle with bread crumb mixture. Broil 1 minute. Sprinkle with mozzarella; broil until cheese is golden, 1 to 2 minutes longer; serve.

PER SERVING: 427 Cal., 19g Fat (8g Sat.), 92mg Chol., 2g Fiber, 42g Pro., 22g Carb., 1,021mg Sod.

Lemony Chicken Breasts with Rice

Prep: 10 min.
Cook: 3 hr.
Serves: 4
Cost per serving:
$2.25

- 4 Tbsp. unsalted butter
- 1 onion, finely chopped
- 2 garlic cloves, finely chopped
- 4 boneless, skinless chicken breast halves
- Salt and pepper
- 4 cups low-sodium chicken broth
- ¼ cup lemon juice
- 2 cups long-grain rice
- ¼ cup finely chopped fresh parsley

1 Melt 2 Tbsp. butter in a large skillet over medium-high heat. Add onion and cook until softened, stirring occasionally, 4 to 5 minutes. Add garlic and sauté 1 minute longer. Scrape into slow cooker.

2 Sprinkle chicken with salt. Melt remaining 2 Tbsp. butter in skillet over medium-high heat until foaming. Add chicken breast halves and cook until browned, about 2 minutes per side. Transfer to slow cooker.

3 Add 1 cup broth and lemon juice to skillet and bring to a boil, scraping browned bits from bottom of pan. Add to slow cooker, along with remaining broth, rice and 1 tsp. salt. Stir, cover and cook on low until chicken is cooked through and rice is tender, 2 to 3 hours. Remove chicken, stir parsley into rice and season with salt and pepper. Divide rice onto 4 plates and top each with a piece of chicken; serve immediately.

PER SERVING: 534 Cal., 15g Fat (8g Sat.), 54mg Chol., 2g Fiber, 20g Pro., 80g Carb., 323mg Sod.

✳ SMART TIP
✳ **Chop the chicken.** You can serve the chicken in large pieces or slice it up for a different look.

Curried Chicken and Chickpea Stew

Prep: 15 min.
Cook: 8 hr.
Serves: 8
Cost per serving:

$1.57

- 1½ lb. boneless, skinless chicken breasts, cut into 2-inch pieces
- 1½ lb. boneless, skinless chicken thighs, cut into 2-inch pieces
- 1 Tbsp. olive oil
- 1 Tbsp. curry powder
- ½ tsp. salt
- 2 onions, thinly sliced
- 4 cloves garlic, finely chopped
- 1 28-oz. can diced tomatoes with juice
- 2 15-oz. cans chickpeas, rinsed and drained

1 Combine chicken, olive oil, curry powder and salt in slow cooker and stir to coat.

2 Sprinkle onions and garlic on top of chicken. Pour tomatoes and juice on top. Cover and cook on low for 6 to 8 hours.

3 During last hour of cooking time, stir chickpeas into stew. Serve hot.

PER SERVING: 327 Cal., 7g Fat (1g Sat.), 120mg Chol., 4g Fiber, 42g Pro., 22g Carb., 823mg Sod.

RYAN BENYI, FOOD STYLING: LYNN MILLER

Tortilla Soup

SMART TIPS

❋ **Serve with condiments.** Offer bowls of sour cream, diced avocado, chopped scallions, salsa, extra chips and lime wedges on the side.

❋ **Go meatless.** For a vegetarian alternative, skip the chicken and use canned beans (such as pinto) instead. Swap vegetable broth for the chicken broth.

❋ **Add some heat.** For a spicy soup, cook a chopped, seeded jalapeño chili with the onion, and add a dash or two of hot sauce when you stir in the broth.

Prep: 5 min.
Cook: 25 min.
Serves: 4
Cost per serving:

$1.90

- 1 Tbsp. vegetable oil
- 1 small onion, finely chopped
- 2 cloves garlic, finely chopped
- 1½ tsp. chili powder
- ¼ tsp. crushed red pepper
- 32 oz. low-sodium chicken broth
- 1 14.5-oz. can diced tomatoes
- 2 cups shredded skinless cooked chicken (from a rotisserie chicken)
- Salt
- 2 Tbsp. fresh cilantro leaves
- 4 oz. corn tortilla chips

1 Warm vegetable oil in a large pot over medium heat. Add onion and cook, stirring frequently, until softened, about 5 minutes. Add garlic, chili powder and crushed red pepper; cook mixture for 30 seconds, stirring constantly.

2 Stir broth and tomatoes into pot and bring soup to a boil. Reduce heat to low and simmer 15 minutes. Stir in chicken and cook until heated through, 1 to 2 minutes, stirring occasionally. Season with salt. Stir in cilantro. Divide tortilla chips among 4 soup bowls. Ladle soup on top of chips and serve immediately.

PER SERVING: 331 Cal., 13g Fat (2g Sat.), 60mg Chol., 3g Fiber, 28g Pro., 27g Carb., 1,319mg Sod.

Creamy Chicken and Broccoli Curry

Prep: 10 min.
Cook: 20 min.
Serves: 4
Cost per serving:

$2.25

- 1½ lb. boneless, skinless chicken breast tenders
- Salt and pepper
- ¼ cup all-purpose flour
- 3 Tbsp. vegetable oil
- 1 large onion, coarsely chopped
- 1½ tsp. hot (madras) curry powder
- 14 oz. chicken broth
- 10 oz. frozen broccoli florets, thawed
- ½ cup sour cream

1 Place tenders in a large bowl; sprinkle ½ tsp. salt and ¼ tsp. pepper on top. Add flour and stir to coat chicken.

2 In a large nonstick skillet, warm half of oil over medium-high heat. Add half of chicken and cook, turning once or twice, until golden on both sides, about 4 minutes. Transfer chicken to a plate and repeat using remaining oil and chicken tenders.

3 Add onion, curry powder, and ¼ tsp. each salt and pepper to pan and cook, stirring, until onion softens, about 5 minutes. Add broth and bring to a boil. Reduce heat and simmer until sauce is reduced by half, 3 to 4 minutes. Return chicken to pan and cook, turning, for 2 minutes. Add broccoli and cook, stirring, for 1 to 2 minutes.

4 Using a slotted spoon, transfer chicken and broccoli to plates. Remove skillet from heat and stir in sour cream. Spoon sauce on top of chicken.

PER SERVING: 416 Cal., 20g Fat (6g Sat.), 119mg Chol., 3g Fiber, 43g Pro., 15g Carb., 1,038mg Sod.

Crunchy Pecan-Crusted Chicken Fingers

Prep: 15 min.
Cook: 20 min.
Serves: 4
Cost per serving:

$1.73

- 16 saltines
- ¼ cup chopped pecans
- 1 tsp. salt
- 2 tsp. paprika
- ¼ cup all-purpose flour
- 1 large egg
- 1½ lb. boneless, skinless chicken breast halves, cut into uniform strips

1 Preheat oven to 425°F. Line a broiler pan with foil. Mist a wire rack with cooking spray and place on top of lined broiler pan.

2 Combine saltines, pecans, salt and paprika in bowl of a food processor and pulse to finely grind and mix. Transfer mixture to a shallow bowl.

3 Place flour in a second shallow bowl. Lightly beat together egg and 1 Tbsp. water in a third shallow bowl.

4 Coat each chicken strip in flour. Dip chicken strips in egg, allowing excess to drip off. Dredge in cracker mixture. Arrange chicken on rack and bake until golden brown, 18 to 20 minutes.

PER SERVING: 301 Cal., 9g Fat (2g Sat.), 152mg Chol., 1g Fiber, 43g Pro., 10g Carb., 753mg Sod.

SMART TIP

❋ **Try panko.**
Japanese bread crumbs, called *panko*, are available at most supermarkets. Coarser than most ordinary store-bought bread crumbs, they make for a lighter, crunchier coating. Use the same amount as with regular bread crumbs.

Buttermilk Chicken Tenders

Prep: 20 min.
Marinate: 1 hr.
Cook: 12 min.
Serves: 6
Cost per serving:

$1.28

- ½ cup buttermilk
- ¾ tsp. Tabasco sauce
- 1⅓ lb. boneless, skinless chicken breast tenders
- ¾ cup all-purpose flour
- 2 tsp. salt
- ⅛ tsp. cayenne pepper
- 2 large eggs
- 2 cups bread crumbs
- ¾ cup vegetable oil

1 Mix buttermilk and Tabasco in a ziplock bag. Add chicken tenders and marinate in refrigerator for at least 1 hour or up to 1 day.

2 Preheat oven to 225°F. In a shallow dish, mix flour with salt and cayenne pepper. In a shallow bowl, beat eggs with 2 Tbsp. water.

Place bread crumbs in a separate shallow dish. Line a baking sheet with waxed paper.

3 Remove chicken from buttermilk, draining any excess, and dredge in flour mixture, shaking off excess; then dip into egg. Next, dip chicken in bread crumbs, pressing gently into crumbs to coat. Place on baking sheet. (Chicken may be prepared up to 5 hours ahead; cover and refrigerate.)

4 In a large skillet, warm ¼ cup vegetable oil over medium-high heat. When hot, add ⅓ of chicken tenders and cook, turning, until golden, about 4 minutes. Transfer to a baking sheet and keep warm. Wipe out pan and repeat in 2 more batches with remaining oil and chicken.
PER SERVING: 467 Cal., 32g Fat (5g Sat.), 131mg Chol., 1g Fiber, 29g Pro., 18g Carb., 606mg Sod.

CHARLES SCHILLER, FOOD STYLING: TRACEY SEAMAN

Chicken Fried Rice with Vegetables

Prep: 7 min.
Cook: 15 min.
Serves: 4
Cost per serving:

96¢

- 1 chicken breast half (about 6 oz.), chopped
- 2 Tbsp. soy sauce
- 2 tsp. sesame oil
- ¼ cup vegetable oil
- ¾ cup chopped onion
- ½ 10-oz. package frozen mixed vegetables, thawed
- 4 cups cooked white rice
- 3 large eggs
- Salt and pepper

1 In a medium bowl, toss chicken with soy sauce and sesame oil. Cover and marinate at room temperature for 10 minutes.

2 Warm a large nonstick skillet over medium-high heat. Add chicken and marinade and stir-fry until chicken is cooked through, 3 to 4 minutes. Transfer chicken to a plate; set aside. Add vegetable oil to skillet and warm over medium heat. Add onion and cook, stirring, for 3 minutes. Stir in vegetables and sauté for 1 minute. Increase heat to medium-high, stir in rice and sauté until incorporated and cooked through, about 3 minutes.

3 Using a wooden spoon, form a well in mixture. Add eggs and scramble within well just until soft. Break apart eggs and mix into rice; season with salt and pepper. Let cook undisturbed until a golden crust forms, about 1 minute. Turn rice with a spatula and cook other side. Repeat 2 or 3 times until rice is uniformly golden. Add chicken and stir to combine. Serve warm.

PER SERVING: 516 Cal., 23g Fat (4g Sat.), 211mg Chol., 2g Fiber, 31g Pro., 49g Carb., 593mg Sod.

SMART TIP

❋ Buy take-out rice. To save time, pick up a quart of cooked rice at a local Chinese restaurant. Break apart any clumps with slightly wet hands.

MARK FERRI; FOOD STYLING: STEPHANIE MALONEY

Individual meat loaves (page 68) bake in just 25 minutes, so they're great for weeknights.

Beef and Lamb

After a long day, there are few things as comforting as coming home to the smell of a hearty supper, and it's especially hard to beat the aroma of steak or meat loaf. With so many cuts of beef and lamb available, you can find a recipe to fit every taste, budget and schedule, whether you're grilling outside or baking a casserole. If you want to get everyone to the table on the double, try one of these meaty dishes.

56 Oven-Baked Mexican Meatballs

57 Orange Beef and Broccoli Stir-Fry

58 Sweet-and-Sour Brisket

59 Beef-and-Pasta Casserole

61 Skirt Steak with Chimichurri

61 Roast Beef and Romaine Salad

62 Corned Beef and Cabbage

63 Beef Kebabs with Orange Glaze

64 Meat Loaf with Mozzarella, Mushrooms and Pepperoni

65 Beef and Barley Soup

67 Beef-and-Rice-Stuffed Peppers

68 Mini Meat Loaves

69 Rice Noodles with Beef

70 Balsamic-Marinated Flank Steak

71 Tortilla Pie

73 Thai-Marinated Broiled Flank Steak

73 Cincinnati Chili

74 Ancho Chili–Rubbed Flank Steak

75 Slow-Cooker Shepherd's Pie

76 Sirloin Burgers with Mushroom Cream Sauce

77 Easy Spaghetti and Meatballs

79 Lamb Chops with Tahini Sauce

80 Curried Lamb Stew with Carrots

81 Mediterranean Brisket

Oven-Baked Mexican Meatballs

Prep: 10 min.
Bake: 20 min.
Serves: 4
Cost per serving:

$1.30

- 1 lb. ground chuck
- 1 large egg
- 2 Tbsp. tomato paste
- 1 cup plain bread crumbs
- 3 cloves garlic, finely chopped (about 3 tsp.)
- 2 Tbsp. finely chopped cilantro
- 2 tsp. chili powder
- Salt and pepper
- 1 Tbsp. vegetable oil
- ½ chipotle chili (canned in adobo sauce), seeded and finely chopped
- 1 28-oz. can crushed tomatoes

1 Adjust oven rack to middle position and preheat to 475°F. Line a rimmed baking sheet with foil. In a large bowl, combine ground meat, egg, tomato paste, bread crumbs, 2 tsp. garlic, cilantro, chili powder and 1 tsp. salt; mix with your fingers to combine well, but do not overmix. Form mixture into 1½-inch meatballs and place on prepared baking sheet. Mist meatballs with nonstick cooking spray. Bake until meatballs are well browned, 17 to

20 minutes, turning once or twice.

2 Warm oil in a large saucepan over medium-low heat. Add remaining 1 tsp. garlic and cook until fragrant, about 1 minute. Add chili and cook, stirring, for 30 seconds. Add tomatoes, bring to a simmer and cook until

slightly thickened, about 10 minutes, stirring occasionally. Season with salt and pepper. Transfer meatballs to saucepan, gently stir to coat with sauce, and serve immediately.

PER SERVING: 403 Cal., 18g Fat (6g Sat.), 126mg Chol., 4g Fiber, 30g Pro., 30g Carb., 966mg Sod.

SMART TIP

✳ Adjust the heat. Canned chipotles vary in spiciness by brand, so use a small piece in the sauce to start. You can always add more if you like it spicier.

CHARLES SCHILLER; FOOD STYLING: TARA BENCH

SMART TIPS

✳ Freshen it up.
Swap fresh broccoli for frozen; cook it in boiling salted water for 2 minutes first.

✳ Get creative.
To dress up this dish, toss in chopped fresh ginger, sliced scallions, strips of red and yellow bell peppers or slivered snow peas while stir-frying.

✳ Intensify the flavor. If time permits, marinate the beef overnight in a mixture of orange zest, chopped fresh thyme, a crushed clove of garlic and olive oil. Be sure to pat the meat dry before starting to cook the stir-fry.

Orange Beef and Broccoli Stir-Fry

Prep: 5 min.
Cook: 7 min.
Serves: 4
Cost per serving:

$2.12

- ¼ cup low-sodium beef broth or water
- 1 Tbsp. soy sauce
- 1 Tbsp. lemon juice
- 2 tsp. cornstarch
- 1 Tbsp. vegetable oil
- 1 lb. top round London broil, cut into strips
- 1 10-oz. package frozen broccoli spears, thawed and patted dry
- 1 Tbsp. grated orange zest
- ¼ cup fresh orange juice
- Salt and pepper

1 Whisk together broth, soy sauce, lemon juice and cornstarch in a bowl; set aside.

2 Warm oil in a wok or large skillet over medium-high heat until hot. Add beef, turn heat to high and cook, stirring constantly, until meat is no longer pink, 2 to 3 minutes.

3 Add broccoli and cook, stirring, until warmed through, about 2 minutes.

4 Stir in reserved sauce, orange zest and juice. Cook, stirring constantly and vigorously, until sauce is thickened, about 2 minutes. Season with salt and pepper.

PER SERVING: 227 Cal., 10g Fat (3g Sat.), 37mg Chol., 2g Fiber, 27g Pro., 7g Carb., 304mg Sod.

Sweet-and-Sour Brisket

Prep: 5 min.
Cook: 6 hr.
Serves: 6
Cost per serving:

$2.12

- **1 28-oz. can crushed tomatoes**
- **1 onion, thinly sliced**
- **2 cloves garlic, finely chopped**
- **½ cup raisins, optional**
- **¼ cup packed light brown sugar**
- **2 Tbsp. fresh lemon juice**
- **1 2½-lb. piece flat-cut brisket, trimmed**
- **Salt and pepper**

1 Place tomatoes, onion, garlic, raisins (if using), brown sugar and lemon juice in a slow cooker and stir to combine. Season brisket with salt and pepper. Place brisket on tomato mixture; spoon half of mixture over meat. Cover and cook on high until meat is fork-tender, 5 to 6 hours.

2 Transfer brisket to a cutting board, tent with foil to keep warm, and let stand for 10 minutes. Skim fat from sauce and discard; season sauce with salt and pepper. Slice brisket across grain, transfer to a serving platter and spoon sauce over meat.

PER SERVING: 355 Cal., 13g Fat (4g Sat.), 99mg Chol., 2g Fiber, 41g Pro., 17g Carb., 372mg Sod.

CHARLES SCHILLER; FOOD STYLING: LYNN MILLER

Beef-and-Pasta Casserole

SMART TIPS

✳ **Choose the right vessel.** A Dutch oven works wonders for this recipe since it can go from stovetop to broiler to table. Look for a deep pot with a heavy bottom.

✳ **Use your shears.** To chop up canned stewed tomatoes the easy way, cut the tomatoes in the can using kitchen scissors.

Prep: 5 min.
Cook: 30 min.
Serves: 6
Cost per serving:
$1.92

- Salt and pepper
- 8 oz. rotini pasta
- ½ cup plain, dry bread crumbs
- ⅓ cup grated Parmesan
- 1½ Tbsp. olive oil
- 1 small onion, finely chopped
- 1 clove garlic, minced
- 1½ lb. lean ground beef
- 1 28-oz. can stewed tomatoes, broken up
- ½ tsp. dried oregano
- 1½ cups shredded Cheddar

1. In a large pot of boiling salted water, cook pasta, stirring occasionally, until al dente, about 10 minutes. Drain and set aside. In a bowl, mix bread crumbs and Parmesan; set aside.

2. In a 3-quart ovenproof pot, warm oil over medium heat. Add onion and garlic and sauté for 4 minutes. Increase heat to medium-high, add ground beef and cook, stirring, until beef is well browned, about 7 minutes. Scrape beef into a colander to drain off excess fat. Wipe out pot and return beef to pot; reduce heat to medium.

3. Preheat broiler. Stir tomatoes, salt, oregano and pepper into beef and cook for 3 minutes. Add reserved pasta and mix. Cook for 2 to 3 minutes to heat pasta. Remove from heat and stir in Cheddar.

4. Top pasta with reserved bread-crumb mixture and cook under broiler until golden brown, 2 to 3 minutes. Serve immediately.

PER SERVING: 554 Cal., 23g Fat (10g Sat.), 71mg Chol., 3g Fiber, 38g Pro., 46g Carb., 1,139mg Sod.

CHARLES SCHILLER

Skirt Steak with Chimichurri

Prep: 5 min.
Cook: 10 min.
Serves: 6
Cost per serving:

$2.39

- ½ cup finely chopped fresh parsley
- ⅓ cup extra-virgin olive oil
- ¼ cup fresh lemon juice (from 2 small lemons)
- 2 cloves garlic, finely chopped
- ½ tsp. crushed red pepper, or more to taste
- Salt
- 1½ lb. skirt steak

1 Make chimichurri: In a small bowl, combine parsley, olive oil, lemon juice, garlic, crushed red pepper and ¼ tsp. salt.

2 Prepare steak: Preheat a gas grill to high; oil when hot (alternatively, place a ridged grill pan on stovetop over medium-high heat; oil when hot). Season steak with salt. Grill steak for 4 to 6 minutes, turn over and continue to cook until done, 3 to 4 minutes more for medium-rare, depending on thickness of meat and heat of grill (you can grill on stovetop for same amount of time).

3 Transfer steak to a cutting board. Tent it loosely with foil and let stand for 5 minutes. Using a sharp knife, slice steak thinly, taking care to cut across grain. Spoon chimichurri on top of steak and serve immediately.

PER SERVING: 339 Cal., 23g Fat (6g Sat.), 67mg Chol., 0g Fiber, 31g Pro., 2g Carb., 161mg Sod.

SMART TIPS

✳ **Try a different steak.** Can't find skirt steak at your grocery store? Swap in hanger steak instead.

✳ **Top things off.** Chimichurri, a traditional Argentinian herb sauce, is delicious spooned over beef. You can make it up to 2 hours ahead; cover and refrigerate.

Roast Beef and Romaine Salad

Prep: 10 min.
Serves: 4
Cost per serving:

$2.29

- ¼ cup low-fat plain yogurt
- ¼ cup light mayonnaise
- 1½ Tbsp. lemon juice
- Salt and pepper
- ½ cup crumbled blue cheese (2 oz.)
- 2 heads romaine lettuce, quartered lengthwise and cut crosswise into ½-inch strips (about 9 cups)
- 8 oz. thinly sliced roast beef, cut into small pieces
- 1 cup croutons

1 Make dressing: Whisk together yogurt, mayonnaise, lemon juice, salt, pepper and 2 Tbsp. water in a small bowl. Stir in blue cheese.

2 Place romaine in large bowl and toss with dressing to coat. Add roast beef and croutons, and gently toss again. Serve immediately.

PER SERVING: 195 Cal., 7g Fat (3g Sat.), 37mg Chol., 3g Fiber, 20g Pro., 16g Carb., 955mg Sod.

SMART TIPS

✳ **Cut the fat.** Trim most of the fat from the brisket before cooking. As the meat cooks, the water turns into a flavorful, but not greasy, broth for the vegetables.

✳ **Enjoy leftovers.** If you have leftover corned beef, wrap it well and keep it refrigerated. Serve the leftovers hot or cold, deli style—on rye bread slathered with grainy mustard.

Corned Beef and Cabbage

Prep: 5 min.
Cook: 8½ hr.
Serves: 6
Cost per serving:

$2.40

- 1½ lb. small red potatoes
- 4 cloves garlic, left whole
- 1 4-lb. corned beef

brisket with seasoning packet, rinsed and trimmed
- 2 whole cloves
- 1 small onion
- 24 baby carrots
- 1 small white cabbage, cut into 8 wedges

1 Arrange potatoes and garlic on bottom of slow cooker. Place corned beef on top of potatoes and sprinkle evenly with seasoning from packet. Push cloves into onion and add to slow cooker. Add enough water to slow cooker to just cover meat. Cover and cook on low until meat is tender, 6½ to 8 hours.

2 Transfer meat to cutting board and cover with foil to keep warm. Transfer potatoes to bowl and cover with foil to keep warm. Add carrots and cabbage to slow cooker, turn to high, cover and cook until vegetables are just tender, about 30 minutes.

3 Using a sharp knife, slice corned beef across grain and serve with potatoes, carrots and cabbage.

PER SERVING: 560 Cal., 19g Fat (8g Sat.), 216mg Chol., 5g Fiber, 68g Pro., 30g Carb., 2,561mg Sod.

CHARLES SCHILLER, FOOD STYLING: LYNN MILLER

Beef Kebabs with Orange Glaze

Prep: 15 min.
Cook: 10 min.
Yield: 8 kebabs
Cost per serving:

89¢

- ¼ cup frozen orange juice concentrate
- ¼ cup soy sauce
- 2 tsp. Dijon mustard
- 4 Tbsp. unsalted butter, melted
- 1½ lb. boneless sirloin, cut into 1-inch cubes
- 8 mushrooms, halved
- 1 red onion, quartered, layers separated
- ½ pint cherry tomatoes
- Salt and pepper

1 Preheat broiler or prepare a charcoal fire and let burn to a gray ash. Stir orange juice concentrate with soy sauce, mustard and butter in a small saucepan over medium-high heat until smooth, about 2 minutes.

2 Thread beef cubes onto 8 long metal skewers, dividing evenly and alternating with mushrooms, onion pieces and tomatoes. Brush orange mixture evenly over beef and vegetables and season generously with salt and pepper. Pour any remaining glaze into a saucepan and bring to a boil, then remove from heat and reserve.

3 Set broiling pan or grill about 6 inches from heat source. Broil or grill skewers, turning often, until meat and mushrooms are browned and onions and tomatoes are just charred on edges, about 7 minutes. Serve kebabs hot, passing reserved warmed glaze on the side.

PER SERVING (1 KEBAB): 253 Cal., 17g Fat (8g Sat.), 72mg Chol., 1g Fiber, 19g Pro., 8g Carb., 326mg Sod.

SMART TIP

✳ **Take a rest.** To get juicy meat, let kebabs stand for 5 minutes before serving.

Meat Loaf with Mozzarella, Mushrooms and Pepperoni

Prep: 10 min.
Cook: 5 hr.
Serves: 6
Cost per serving:

$1.99

- 2 slices white sandwich bread
- 1½ lb. ground sirloin
- 1½ cups finely chopped button mushrooms
- 1 cup shredded part-skim mozzarella
- ⅓ cup finely chopped pepperoni
- 1 tsp. dried oregano
- 1 tsp. garlic powder
- ¾ tsp. salt
- 2 large eggs, lightly beaten
- 2 Tbsp. ketchup

1 Tear bread into large pieces and blend in a food processor until it forms fine crumbs. Combine crumbs, sirloin, mushrooms, mozzarella, pepperoni, oregano, garlic powder, salt and eggs in a large bowl and mix gently with your hands to combine. Form mixture into a 9-by-6-inch loaf. Place in slow cooker.

2 Brush meat loaf with ketchup. Cover and cook on low until meat is cooked through, about 5 hours.

PER SERVING: 297 Cal., 12g Fat (6g Sat.), 154mg Chol., 1g Fiber, 35g Pro., 11g Carb., 655mg Sod.

CHARLES SCHILLER; FOOD STYLING: ANDREA STEINBERG

Beef and Barley Soup

SMART TIPS

Keep leftovers. Freeze extra soup in single-serving containers for up to one month.

Add sides. This classic soup is a meal in a bowl, but a salad and some crusty whole-grain rolls make ideal accompaniments.

Try other veggies. For a different flavor, swap parsnips for the carrots, or use both.

Prep: 15 min.
Cook: 7 hr.
Serves: 8
Cost per serving:

$2.23

- 2 Tbsp. vegetable oil
- 2 onions, chopped
- 10 oz. white button mushrooms, sliced
- 2 lb. lean beef stew meat, cut into ½-inch pieces
- 6 cups low-sodium beef broth
- 2 carrots, chopped
- 1 28-oz. can diced tomatoes with juice
- 1 Tbsp. Worcestershire sauce
- 1 tsp. dried thyme
- ½ tsp. garlic powder
- ⅔ cup pearl barley
- Salt and pepper

1. Warm 1 Tbsp. vegetable oil in a large skillet over medium-high heat. Add onions and mushrooms and cook, stirring frequently, until vegetables have softened slightly and mushrooms have released their liquid, about 7 minutes. Scrape vegetables into slow cooker. Warm remaining 1 Tbsp. vegetable oil in same skillet. Add beef and cook, stirring, until meat is browned on all sides, about 5 minutes. (If skillet is too small, cook beef in batches, adding more oil if needed.) Scrape beef into slow cooker.

2. Pour 1 cup of broth into skillet and stir with a wooden spoon to scrape up any browned bits on bottom of pan. Pour broth from skillet, remaining broth, carrots, tomatoes, Worcestershire sauce, thyme, garlic powder, barley and 1 tsp. salt into slow cooker. Stir, cover and cook on low until meat is tender, 6 to 7 hours. Season with salt and pepper and serve hot.

PER SERVING: 448 Cal., 28g Fat (10g Sat.), 82mg Chol., 4g Fiber, 26g Pro., 24g Carb., 899mg Sod.

Beef-and-Rice-Stuffed Peppers

Prep: 15 min.
Cook: 32 min.
Serves: 6
Cost per serving:

$2.02

- 6 medium bell peppers, tops removed and reserved, and seeds removed
- 1 Tbsp. olive oil
- 1 yellow onion, diced
- 1 large carrot, diced
- 1 stalk celery, diced
- 2 cloves garlic, minced
- 8 oz. lean (90 percent) ground beef
- 1 tsp. salt
- 1 tsp. pepper
- 1 14.5-oz. can diced tomatoes
- 1 cup cooked brown rice
- 1 cup grated Monterey Jack

1 Preheat oven to 375°F. Bring a large pot of water to a boil. Once boiling, add peppers and pepper tops and cook until tender, 6 to 7 minutes. Remove peppers from water and invert to drain fully.

2 Make filling: Warm olive oil in a large skillet over medium-high heat. Add onion and cook, stirring occasionally, until translucent, about 4 minutes. Add carrot, celery and garlic and continue cooking and stirring until vegetables are just softened, 4 minutes longer. Add beef, salt and pepper and cook, breaking up large chunks, until meat is no longer pink, about 7 minutes. Add tomatoes and rice and cook 5 minutes longer. Stir in ¾ cup cheese.

3 Fill peppers with meat mixture, dividing evenly. Sprinkle mixture with remaining cheese and top with pepper lid. Bake until cheese is melted and peppers are heated through, about 5 minutes. Serve hot.

PER SERVING: 240 Cal., 12g Fat (6g Sat.), 33mg Chol., 5g Fiber, 12g Pro., 23g Carb., 688mg Sod.

SMART TIPS

✳ **Speed it up.** Use leftover cooked rice for this recipe, or microwave instant rice.

✳ **Turn up the heat.** Replace Monterey Jack with pepper Jack for a spicy kick. Instead of plain diced tomatoes, choose a variety that has roasted garlic or diced green chilies in it.

CHOP ONIONS LIKE A PRO

Prep them as quickly as your favorite star chefs with this handy step-by-step guide.

1 **Peel them.** As you peel each onion, cut off the stem end (leave the root end intact). Cut a sliver off one side so the onion won't roll.

2 **Make cuts.** Using a sharp chef's knife, make several vertical cuts from the root end, leaving the root intact. Holding the onion together, carefully make horizontal cuts through the onion, still leaving the root intact.

3 **Give them a chop.** Pushing down on the knife's heel, chop from top to bottom.

Mini Meat Loaves

Prep: 10 min.
Bake: 25 min.
Serves: 4
Cost per serving:

$1.94

- ¼ cup ketchup
- 2 Tbsp. light brown sugar
- 1 Tbsp. Dijon mustard
- 1½ lb. ground beef chuck
- 1 cup plain bread crumbs
- 1 cup canned tomato sauce
- 1 large egg, lightly beaten
- 4 tsp. dried basil
- 1 tsp. garlic powder
- 1 tsp. onion powder
- Salt and pepper

1 Line a broiler pan with aluminum foil and place it in oven. Preheat oven to 425°F. Whisk together ketchup, brown sugar and mustard in a small bowl and set aside.

2 In a large bowl, combine ground beef, bread crumbs, tomato sauce, egg, basil, garlic powder, onion powder, salt and pepper. Blend with your fingers until well combined, but do not overmix. Divide mixture into 4 equal portions and shape each into a mini loaf. Each will be about 4 inches long and 3 inches wide.

3 Brush each meat loaf with some ketchup mixture. Remove pan from oven and mist with nonstick cooking spray. Carefully transfer meat loaves to hot broiler pan. Bake until an instant-read thermometer inserted into center of a loaf registers 160°F,

20 to 25 minutes. Remove loaves from oven and let stand on broiler pan for 2 to 3 minutes. Using a wide spatula, carefully transfer each meat loaf to a plate. Serve immediately.
PER SERVING: 621 Cal., 37g Fat (14g Sat.), 175mg Chol., 2g Fiber, 36g Pro., 35g Carb., 900mg Sod.

SMART TIP

✳ **Eye portions.** Each loaf serves 1 adult or 2 children who have smaller appetites. If you have leftovers, wrap tightly and refrigerate or freeze.

CHARLES SCHILLER; FOOD STYLING: LYNN MILLER

SMART TIPS

✳ **Use your noodle.** Rice-stick noodles are available in the ethnic or Asian foods section of many supermarkets. If you can't find them in your grocery store, feel free to swap in angel hair pasta.

✳ **Go shopping in your fridge.** If you have leftover steak, use it in this dish instead of cooking fresh meat. Same goes for vegetables—toss in last night's broccoli or green beans.

Rice Noodles with Beef

Prep: 20 min.
Cook: 10 min.
Serves: 6
Cost per serving:

$2.24

- 1 8-oz. package pad Thai rice-stick noodles
- 1 1-lb. bag frozen Asian stir-fry vegetables
- 2 cloves garlic, minced
- 1 1-inch piece fresh ginger, grated
- 1½ Tbsp. soy sauce
- 1 Tbsp. red curry paste
- 1 Tbsp. rice wine vinegar
- 2 Tbsp. lime juice
- 5 Tbsp. peanut oil
- 1 lb. beef sirloin or flank steak, sliced ¼-inch thick
- 1 red bell pepper, sliced into ¼-inch strips
- 6 scallions, sliced (1 cup)
- ½ lb. bean sprouts (2 cups), optional
- ½ cup roasted, unsalted peanuts, chopped, optional

1 In a large bowl filled with cold water, soak rice noodles until softened, about 15 minutes; drain. Add to a pot of boiling water and cook for 5 minutes. Drain again and set noodles aside.

2 Rinse Asian vegetables in a colander briefly with cold water; let drain thoroughly. In a small bowl, stir together garlic, ginger, soy sauce, curry paste, vinegar, lime juice and 2 Tbsp. peanut oil; set aside.

3 In a large, nonstick skillet, warm 1 Tbsp. peanut oil over medium-high heat. Add half of beef and stir-fry for 4 minutes. Transfer to a plate. Repeat process with 1 Tbsp. oil and remaining beef. Cover beef to keep warm. Wipe out pan; add remaining 1 Tbsp. oil and bell pepper; stir-fry for 2 minutes. Add scallions and reserved Asian vegetables and stir-fry for 3 minutes.

4 Add reserved sauce to skillet; cook for 1 minute. Add beef and cooked noodles and toss thoroughly to combine with sauce.

5 Serve noodles in bowls topped with bean sprouts and peanuts, if desired.

PER SERVING: 380 Cal., 15g Fat (3g Sat.), 46mg Chol., 2g Fiber, 21g Pro., 40g Carb., 378mg Sod.

Balsamic-Marinated Flank Steak

Prep: 5 min.
Chill: 20 min.
Cook: 15 min.
Serves: 6
Cost per serving:

$2.02

- ½ cup balsamic vinegar
- 1 Tbsp. packed light brown sugar
- 1 tsp. dried rosemary
- Salt and pepper
- 1½ lb. flank steak

1 Combine vinegar, sugar, rosemary and 1½ tsp. salt in a ziplock bag. Add steak to bag, seal and turn bag several times to coat meat with marinade. Refrigerate 20 minutes, turning once or twice.

2 Preheat a gas grill to high. Remove steak from marinade and sprinkle both sides with salt and pepper. Discard marinade. Grill steak for 4 to 6 minutes, turn over, and continue to grill until done, 3 to 4 minutes more for medium-rare, depending on thickness of meat and heat of grill. (Alternatively, grill steak on a lightly oiled ridged grill pan over medium-high heat on stove, for same amount of time.)

3 Transfer steak to cutting board, tent loosely with foil and let stand 5 minutes before slicing and serving.

PER SERVING: 199 Cal., 8g Fat (4g Sat.), 57mg Chol., 0g Fiber, 23g Pro., 5g Carb., 471mg Sod.

RYAN BENYI, FOOD STYLING: STEPHANA BOTTOM

Tortilla Pie

SMART TIPS

✽ **Offer sides.** Serve bowls of extra salsa or pico de gallo, sour cream, chopped scallions, sliced avocado and lime wedges.

✽ **Make individual pies.** You can make smaller versions so everyone can have their own—simply use taco-sized tortillas. For a different taste, try corn instead of flour.

Prep: 20 min.
Bake: 12 min.
Serves: 4
Cost per serving:

$2.42

- 4 10-inch flour tortillas
- 2 tsp. vegetable oil
- 1 small onion, chopped
- 3 cloves garlic, chopped
- 1 Tbsp. chili powder
- 1 tsp. ground cumin
- Salt
- 1 lb. extra-lean ground beef (90 percent)
- ½ cup tomato sauce
- 1 cup green salsa
- 6 oz. grated pepper Jack

1 Preheat oven to 450°F. Place a skillet on the stovetop over high heat. Mist tortillas with cooking spray and toast in skillet, turning once, until golden, about 1 minute.

2 Warm oil in skillet over medium heat. Add onion and sauté for 4 minutes. Stir in garlic, spices and salt; sauté for 1 minute. Add beef and sauté, breaking into small pieces, until cooked, about 5 minutes. Add tomato sauce, reduce heat and simmer until most of liquid has evaporated, about 7 minutes. Drain on a paper towel–lined plate.

3 Place a tortilla on a baking sheet misted with cooking spray. Spread with one-third each of beef mixture, salsa and cheese. Repeat with 2 more layers of tortillas, beef, salsa and cheese. Top with remaining tortilla; press to adhere. Bake 10 to 12 minutes. Let stand for 5 minutes before serving.
PER SERVING: 595 Cal., 27g Fat (12g Sat.), 107mg Chol., 5g Fiber, 42g Pro., 46g Carb., 1,903mg Sod.

CHARLES SCHILLER.

Thai-Marinated Broiled Flank Steak

Prep: 5 min.
Cook: 10 min.
Serves: 6
Cost per serving:

$1.92

- 2 Tbsp. soy sauce
- 2 tsp. fish sauce
- 2 Tbsp. fresh lime juice
- 1 Tbsp. honey
- 1 tsp. crushed red pepper
- 2 cloves garlic, finely chopped
- 1 ½-inch piece fresh ginger, finely chopped
- 1½ lb. flank steak

1 Whisk together soy sauce, fish sauce, lime juice, honey, crushed red pepper, garlic and ginger in a small bowl. Place flank steak in a ziplock bag and add marinade. Turn bag several times to coat. Let stand for 15 minutes at room temperature, turning once or twice.

2 While steak is marinating, preheat broiler. Broil steak until cooked to desired doneness, about 4 minutes per side for medium-rare. Transfer to a cutting board, tent with foil and let stand for 5 minutes. Slice, transfer to a platter, pour any juices from cutting board over sliced meat and serve.
PER SERVING: 194 Cal., 9g Fat (4g Sat.), 57mg Chol., 0g Fiber, 24g Pro., 4g Carb., 368mg Sod.

SMART TIPS

✳ **Swap meats.** Can't find flank steak at your grocery store? Try skirt steak instead.

✳ **Go fish.** Thai fish sauce, also called *nam pla,* is sold in the ethnic or Asian foods section of supermarkets. If your grocer doesn't have it, use additional soy sauce instead.

Cincinnati Chili

Prep: 15 min.
Cook: 8 hr.
Serves: 10
Cost per serving:

$1.05

- 2 lb. lean ground beef
- Salt
- 1 6-oz. can tomato paste
- 2 onions, finely chopped
- 2 cloves garlic, finely chopped
- 2 Tbsp. chili powder
- 2 tsp. dried oregano
- 1 tsp. unsweetened cocoa powder
- 1 tsp. cinnamon
- ½ tsp. allspice
- ½ tsp. cayenne pepper
- 1 15-oz. can kidney beans, rinsed and drained

1 In a large skillet, cook ground beef and 1 tsp. salt over medium-high heat, stirring and breaking up beef with a spoon, until meat loses its pink color, about 8 minutes. Drain excess fat from pan.

2 Add meat to slow cooker along with 2 cups water, tomato paste, onions, garlic, chili powder, oregano, cocoa, cinnamon, allspice and cayenne pepper. Cover and cook on low for 5 to

7 hours. Add beans and cook 1 hour more, stirring in an additional ½ cup water if chili looks dry. Season with salt.
PER SERVING: 225 Cal., 10g Fat (4g Sat.), 59mg Chol., 4g Fiber, 21g Pro., 13g Carb., 365mg Sod.

SMART TIP

✳ **Put it on top.** Serve the chili as Ohioans do: over spaghetti.

KANA OKADA, FOOD STYLING: SUSAN VAJARANANT

CHICKEN & TURKEY

BEEF & LAMB

PORK

FISH

VEGETABLES

SMART TIPS

✳ Give it a kick.
Ancho chili powder has a slightly sweet flavor and is very mild, so it adds just a touch of spice. Toss in ¼ to ½ teaspoon cayenne if you want to turn up the heat.

✳ Keep an eye on it.
Flank steak is lean but very tender, and it works great on the grill. But be sure not to overcook it, or it will get very tough.

Ancho Chili–Rubbed Flank Steak

Prep: 5 min.
Cook: 10 min.
Serves: 8
Cost per serving:

$2.38

- 1 Tbsp. ancho chili powder
- ¼ tsp. cinnamon
- 2 cloves garlic, chopped
- 2 tsp. ground cumin
- 1 tsp. onion powder
- ½ tsp. salt
- ¼ tsp. pepper
- 2 flank steaks, about 1¼ lb. each

1 Preheat broiler or prepare a medium-hot charcoal fire. In a small bowl, combine chili powder, cinnamon, garlic, cumin, onion powder, salt and pepper. Stir to combine and set aside.

2 Arrange steaks on a work surface. Using a sharp knife, make several small shallow incisions along surface of each steak, cutting against the grain. Rub chili mixture into both sides of steaks.

3 Broil or grill steaks about 6 inches from heat source for 4 to 5 minutes per side (for medium-rare). Remove steaks to a cutting board and let stand for 5 minutes. Using a sharp knife, cut against the grain into thin slices.
PER SERVING: 177 Cal., 7g Fat (3g Sat.), 48mg Chol., 1g Fiber, 25g Pro., 1g Carb., 221mg Sod.

JOHN MONTANA, FOOD STYLING: LYNN MILLER

Slow-Cooker Shepherd's Pie

Prep: 10 min.
Cook: 3½ hr.
Serves: 6
Cost per serving:

$1.39

- **4 medium Yukon gold potatoes (about 2 lb.)**
- **⅓ cup milk**
- **2 Tbsp. unsalted butter**
- **Salt and pepper**
- **1 Tbsp. olive oil**
- **1 medium onion, diced**
- **2 cloves garlic, minced**
- **1 lb. lean ground beef**
- **1 tsp. Worcestershire sauce**
- **1 Tbsp. tomato paste**
- **1 tsp. dried thyme**
- **1 Tbsp. cornstarch**
- **1 cup frozen mixed vegetables**

1 Prick potatoes all over with a fork. Microwave potatoes on high, turning once, until tender, about 15 minutes. Remove from microwave, let cool slightly, then peel and mash with milk and butter. Season with salt and pepper.

2 In a skillet over medium heat, warm olive oil. Add onion and cook, stirring, until translucent, about 3 minutes. Add garlic and sauté 30 seconds longer.

Add beef, increase heat to medium-high and cook, breaking up chunks, until meat is cooked through and beginning to brown, about 8 minutes. Stir in Worcestershire, tomato paste, thyme and ½ tsp. each salt and pepper. In a small cup, whisk cornstarch with 1 cup water. Add to skillet and

cook, stirring, until liquid thickens slightly. Remove from heat; transfer to slow cooker.

3 Layer vegetables on top of meat; top with potatoes. Cover, turn slow cooker to low and cook for 3 hours.

PER SERVING: 353 Cal., 14g Fat (6g Sat.), 61mg Chol., 3g Fiber, 20g Pro., 34g Carb., 398mg Sod.

SMART TIP

✳ **Make it ahead.** You can prepare the ingredients and layer the shepherd's pie the night before you want to serve it. Cover and refrigerate, then cook it the following day.

CHARLES SCHILLER; FOOD STYLING: STEPHANA BOTTOM

Sirloin Burgers with Mushroom Cream Sauce

SMART TIPS

✻ **Don't mind the many mushrooms.** They'll cook down when their liquid is released in the skillet. (If you have small kids, invite them to watch—they might get a kick out of seeing the mushrooms shrink.)

✻ **Round out the meal.** Serve creamy mashed potatoes and a green veggie such as broccoli or a salad to accompany this satisfying dish.

Prep: 5 min.
Cook: 27 min.
Serves: 4
Cost per serving:

$2.35

- 1½ lb. ground sirloin
- Salt and pepper
- 2 Tbsp. vegetable oil
- 1 small onion, diced

- 10 oz. mushrooms, sliced (4 cups)
- ½ cup heavy cream
- 2 Tbsp. chopped fresh parsley

1 Mix sirloin, salt and pepper. Form 4 thick burgers that are about 4 inches wide.

2 Warm oil in a large skillet over medium-high heat. Cook burgers until browned, about 5 minutes per side. Transfer to a plate; cover with foil.

3 Pour off all but 1 Tbsp. fat from skillet. Add onion and cook, stirring, until softened, about 2 minutes. Add mushrooms; continue cooking and stirring until mushrooms have given off their liquid and are soft, about 10 minutes. Stir in cream and cook until slightly thickened, about 2 minutes. Stir in parsley. Return burgers to skillet. Turn a few times over low heat until they are coated in sauce and warmed through, about 3 minutes. Spoon mushrooms on top; serve.

PER SERVING: 420 Cal., 27g Fat (11g Sat.), 145mg Chol., 1g Fiber, 39g Pro., 5g Carb., 1,012mg Sod.

Easy Spaghetti and Meatballs

Prep: 10 min.
Cook: 20 min.
Serves: 6
Cost per serving:
$1.92

- Salt
- 1 lb. spaghetti
- 1 25-oz. jar tomato sauce
- 1½ lb. ground beef
- ½ cup bread crumbs, soaked in ¼ cup milk
- ½ cup grated Parmesan
- ½ cup chopped onion
- ¼ cup chopped fresh parsley
- 1 egg, lightly beaten
- 2 cloves garlic, minced

1 Preheat oven to 375°F. In a large pot of boiling salted water, cook spaghetti, stirring often, until al dente, about 10 minutes, or as package label directs. Drain well in a colander. In a large, wide saucepan or deep skillet, warm tomato sauce over low heat while you proceed.

2 While pasta is cooking, combine beef, soaked bread crumbs, cheese, onion, parsley, egg, garlic and 1½ tsp. salt in a large bowl. Gently form mixture into balls slightly larger than golf balls. (They will shrink as they cook.) Lay meatballs out on two nonstick or oiled baking sheets and bake until nicely browned, about 10 minutes.

3 Using tongs, transfer meatballs from baking sheet into skillet with sauce. Turn to coat. Serve meatballs and sauce on top of spaghetti.

PER SERVING: 754 Cal., 35g Fat (14g Sat.), 139mg Chol., 4g Fiber, 36g Pro., 71g Carb., 1,315mg Sod.

CHARLES SCHILLER; FOOD STYLING: TRACEY SEAMAN

SMART TIP

✳ **Stock up.** Buy ground beef when it's on sale and freeze in 4-ounce portions.

Lamb Chops with Tahini Sauce

Prep: 5 min.
Cook: 15 min.
Serves: 4
Cost per serving:

$1.76

TAHINI SAUCE:
- ¼ cup jarred sesame tahini, well stirred
- 3 Tbsp. fresh lemon juice
- 1 clove garlic, pressed or very finely chopped
- ¼ tsp. ground cumin
- Salt

LAMB:
- 4 shoulder blade lamb chops
- 1 Tbsp. vegetable oil

1. Make sauce: Whisk together tahini, ¼ cup water, lemon juice, garlic, cumin and ½ tsp. salt.

2. Make lamb: Sprinkle chops on both sides with salt. Warm vegetable oil in large skillet over medium-high heat. Add chops and sauté until browned on both sides, 10 to 15 minutes total for medium-rare. Drizzle chops with tahini sauce and serve.

PER SERVING: 307 Cal., 21g Fat (4g Sat.), 76mg Chol., 1g Fiber, 26g Pro., 3g Carb., 421mg Sod.

SMART TIPS

✳ **Make it a meal.** Serve the chops with a salad of spinach and cherry tomatoes for a hearty and well-balanced dinner. Offer fluffy rice on the side as well.

✳ **Consider your options.** Use any extra sauce on sandwiches or salads or as a dip for vegetables.

✳ **Try hummus and more.** Use the leftover jarred tahini to make hummus (whirl tahini in a food processor with canned chickpeas, garlic and lemon juice). Or try swapping it in wherever you normally use peanut butter—on sandwiches, in smoothies, in cookies and in sauces.

✳ **Heat things up.** You can grill or broil these chops. Grill for 6 to 8 minutes (for medium-rare), turning once. To broil, place a rack 5 inches from the heat source, brush meat with oil and broil for 10 to 12 minutes total, turning once.

KEEP YOUR DRIED SPICES TASTING FRESH

Dried herbs and spices eventually lose their punch. Follow these simple steps to make sure they keep their flavor longer.

1 Do a color check.
Spices should be bright and colorful. The more faded or gray they look, the less flavorful they'll taste—so check them

every couple of months and toss any that have lost their luster.

2 Sniff it out.
A strong aroma is a sign that your herbs are still in their prime. Take a small amount of dried herbs from the bottle and crush them in

the palm of your hand with your finger. If the herbs don't smell strong, you probably won't be able to taste them.

3 Handle with care.
Moisture will shorten the shelf life of your spices, so don't shake an open container over a steaming pot. Always measure

your spices with a dry measuring spoon, away from the steam. Keep your spices tightly capped and stored in a cool, dry place when you're not using them.

CHICKEN & TURKEY

BEEF & LAMB

PORK

FISH

VEGETABLES

Curried Lamb Stew with Carrots

Prep: 15 min.
Cook: 3 hr.
Serves: 8
Cost per serving:

$2.19

- 4 lb. boneless lean lamb, from shoulder or leg, cut into 2-inch pieces
- Salt and pepper
- 3 Tbsp. vegetable oil
- 1 onion, chopped
- 3 tsp. curry powder
- ¼ cup all-purpose flour
- 3 cups low-sodium chicken broth
- 6 carrots, cut into chunks
- ½ cup golden raisins

1 Pat lamb dry and season on all sides with salt and pepper. Warm oil in a skillet over medium-high heat. Add lamb and cook, turning often, until browned on all sides, 5 to 7 minutes. (Work in batches if necessary. Do not overcrowd skillet or lamb will not brown properly.) Transfer to a slow cooker.

2 Add onion to skillet and cook, stirring often, until slightly softened, about 3 minutes. Sprinkle curry powder and flour over onion. Cook, stirring, 1 to 2 minutes. (Mixture will be very dry.) Pour in broth, increase heat to high and bring to a boil. Stir to scrape up any browned bits on bottom of skillet. Pour liquid in skillet over lamb in slow cooker. Cover and cook on high for 2 hours. Add carrots and raisins and cook 1 hour longer.

3 Use a slotted spoon to transfer lamb to a serving platter and surround with carrots and raisins. Taste sauce and season with additional salt and pepper as needed. Spoon sauce over lamb and serve immediately.

PER SERVING: 426 Cal., 18g Fat (5g Sat.), 147mg Chol., 2g Fiber, 48g Pro., 17g Carb., 534mg Sod.

SMART TIP

✳ **Give it some color.** Sprinkle the stew with chopped fresh parsley just before serving, if desired. Serve it over white or brown rice, or couscous.

CHARLES SCHILLER; FOOD STYLING: STEPHANA BOTTOM

SMART TIPS

❋ **Serve sides.** Offer pasta, rice, mashed potatoes or a baked potato with the brisket. Don't forget to include a vegetable such as green beans, or toss a simple salad.

❋ **Choose the right olives.** Be sure to use a flavorful type of olive, such as kalamata or Niçoise. Mission olives, although delicious on pizza, are too mild for this dish.

❋ **Be fresh.** You can substitute fresh rosemary for dried. Use 1½ teaspoons, chopped.

Mediterranean Brisket

FRANCES JANISCH, FOOD STYLING: LYNN MILLER

Prep: 5 min.
Cook: 6 hr.
Serves: 6
Cost per serving:

$2.40

- 1 14.5-oz. can diced tomatoes with juice
- ½ cup dry red wine
- 5 garlic cloves, chopped
- ⅓ cup kalamata or other black olives, pitted and chopped
- ½ tsp. dried rosemary
- 1 2½-lb. piece flat-cut brisket, fat trimmed off
- Salt and pepper
- 1 Tbsp. finely chopped fresh parsley

1 Place tomatoes, wine, garlic, olives and rosemary in slow cooker and stir to combine. Sprinkle meat with 1½ tsp. salt and pepper to taste. Place it on top of tomato mixture; spoon half of tomato mixture over meat to cover. Cover and cook on high until fork-tender, 5 to 6 hours.

2 Transfer brisket to a cutting board, tent with foil and let stand for 10 minutes. Skim fat from sauce; season with salt and pepper. Slice brisket across grain and transfer to a serving platter. Spoon some sauce over meat and sprinkle with parsley. Serve brisket with remaining sauce on side.

PER SERVING: 424 Cal., 15g Fat (4g Sat.), 180mg Chol., 1g Fiber, 60g Pro., 5g Carb., 545mg Sod.

Delicious pulled pork
(page 85) couldn't be easier,
thanks to your slow cooker.

Pork

Chops, bacon, ham, sausage—pork comes in so many guises, you could enjoy a different style every night of the week. Watching your calories? Pick up a lean pork loin. Looking for an inexpensive crowd-pleasing dish? Go with bacon. Pork works beautifully for dressed-up dinners (try our Cider-Braised Pork Medallions) and casual weeknight fare as well (like our quick Maple-Glazed Ham Steak).

84 Butternut Squash Ravioli with Pancetta

85 Slow-Cooker Pulled Pork

86 Penne with Ham and Asparagus

87 Pork Chops with Rhubarb Chutney

89 Pea Pancakes with Bacon

89 Baked Ziti with Broccoli and Sausage

90 Maple-Glazed Ham Steak

91 Pork and Hominy Stew

92 Honey-Mustard Ham Steaks

93 Braised Pork Chops with Apples and Onion

95 Soy-Marinated Pork Chops

96 Chili-Lime Pork Tenderloin

97 Tortellini with Ham and Peas

98 Parmesan Pork Cutlets

99 Monte Cristo Sandwiches

101 Penne with Sweet Peas and Prosciutto

101 Salami and Swiss Hoagies

102 Ham and Cheddar Supper Waffles

103 Barbecued-Pork Sliders

104 Fried Rice with Ham and Asparagus

105 Stuffed Smoked Pork Chops

107 Cider-Braised Pork Medallions

107 Three-Bean Chili with Bacon

108 Molasses-and-Mustard-Glazed Ribs

109 White Bean Soup

110 Apricot-Onion Pork Medallions

111 Creamy Corn Chowder

113 Western Frittata

114 Bacon-and-Pea-Stuffed Potatoes

115 Spinach Salad with Chickpeas and Warm Bacon Vinaigrette

116 Pasta Carbonara Frittata

117 Black Bean Soup with Sausage

119 Ham, Swiss and Spinach Quiche

119 Pork and Peanut Stir-Fry

120 Ham and Gruyère Stratas

121 Tandoori Roasted Pork Tenderloin

123 Cheesy Baked Penne with Ham and Broccoli

123 Hearty Minestrone with Shells

Butternut Squash Ravioli with Pancetta

Prep: 1 hr.
Cook: 10 min.
Serves: 6
Cost per serving:

$1.51

- 1 1-lb. butternut squash
- Salt and pepper
- 9 Tbsp. unsalted butter
- ⅓ cup chopped shallot
- 1 tsp. finely chopped sage plus 2 Tbsp. thinly sliced leaves and 8 whole leaves
- ¼ cup ricotta
- ½ cup grated Parmesan
- Pinch of nutmeg
- 48 wonton skins
- 4 slices pancetta, chopped

1 Preheat oven to 450°F. Halve squash; remove seeds. Season with salt and pepper and place, flesh side down, on a baking sheet. Bake until tender and a knife pierces easily, about 40 minutes. Use a spoon to scoop out flesh; puree in a food processor or blender until smooth.

2 Melt 1 Tbsp. butter in a skillet. Add shallot; sauté until tender, 3 minutes. Add chopped sage, squash, ricotta and ¼ cup Parmesan. Season with salt, pepper and nutmeg; sauté for 1 minute. Remove from heat and let cool.

3 Place one wonton skin on work surface, keeping the rest covered with a damp cloth. Brush skin with water and place 1 tsp. squash mixture in center. Place another wrapper on top. Seal with fingers, taking care to push out air bubbles. Use a 3-inch round cookie cutter to cut filled ravioli into circles. Keep finished ravioli covered.

4 In a skillet over medium heat, fry pancetta until crispy, about 5½ minutes. Remove from pan and drain on paper towels. Wipe skillet out.

5 Bring a large pot of salted water to a boil. Melt remaining butter in skillet over very low heat, then add sliced sage. Cook butter and sage until butter turns light golden brown, about 5 minutes; remove from heat. While butter is browning, add ravioli to boiling water, stirring gently so they don't stick together. Cook 4 minutes, then carefully drain.

6 Place 4 ravioli on each plate, top each with 1 Tbsp. browned butter and garnish with ½ Tbsp. Parmesan, some crumbled pancetta and one sage leaf. Serve hot.

PER SERVING: 499 Cal., 28g Fat (15g Sat.), 80mg Chol., 3g Fiber, 15g Pro., 48g Carb., 1,053mg Sod.

CHARLES SCHILLER; FOOD STYLING: LYNN MILLER

SMART TIPS

✱ Make extras. Cook 2 batches. This crowd-pleasing pork keeps for up to 5 days in the refrigerator. It also freezes well—try freezing it in single-serving containers.

✱ Try it with chicken. You can make this flavorful dish with chicken if you prefer. Use 3 pounds boneless, skinless breasts or thighs, or a combo, and cook for 5 hours on low.

Slow-Cooker Pulled Pork

Prep: 10 min.
Cook: 9 hr.
Serves: 6
Cost per serving:

$1.89

- 1 3-lb. boneless pork shoulder, skin removed
- 1 onion, chopped
- ½ cup low-sodium chicken broth or water
- 2 cups bottled or homemade barbecue sauce
- 2 Tbsp. mustard
- 2 Tbsp. honey
- 1 Tbsp. soy sauce
- Salt and pepper

1 Trim pork of any excess fat. Scatter onion over bottom of slow cooker and place pork on top. Add broth, cover and cook on low until very tender, about 8 hours. Remove meat and let cool.

2 When cool enough to handle, pull meat into thin shreds, removing all fat and gristle. Skim excess fat from liquid in slow cooker.

3 Return pulled pork to slow cooker and stir in barbecue sauce, mustard, honey and soy sauce. Season with salt and pepper. Cover and cook for 1 hour longer on low. If desired, serve with hamburger buns and sides of pinto beans, corn, tomatoes and coleslaw.

PER SERVING: 584 Cal., 24g Fat (8g Sat.), 178mg Chol., 1g Fiber, 50g Pro., 38g Carb., 1,192mg Sod.

MARK THOMAS; FOOD STYLING: JOYCE SANGIRARDI

Penne with Ham and Asparagus

Prep: 10 min.
Cook: 30 min.
Serves: 4
Cost per serving:

$2.44

- **1 lb. fresh asparagus, tough ends snapped off, cut into 2-inch pieces**
- **2 yellow squash, cut into 1½-inch pieces (12 oz.)**
- **2 Tbsp. olive oil**
- **Salt and pepper**
- **½ lb. penne**
- **1 cup frozen peas (4 oz.)**
- **¼ lb. sliced ham, cut into thin strips**
- **½ cup heavy cream**
- **1 cup grated Parmesan**

1 Preheat oven to 450°F. Combine asparagus and squash in a large baking dish, toss with oil and season with salt and pepper. Roast, stirring occasionally, until lightly browned, 30 minutes.

2 Cook penne according to package directions. Add peas to pasta cooking water 5 minutes before pasta will be done; drain.

3 Return pasta and peas to pot. Stir in ham and cream. Cover; set aside until pasta has absorbed some cream and ham is warmed through, about 2 minutes.

4 Stir in roasted asparagus and squash. Season with salt and pepper and serve with Parmesan.

PER SERVING: 457 Cal., 20g Fat (8g Sat.), 53mg Chol., 5g Fiber, 17g Pro., 53g Carb., 349mg Sod.

MARK THOMAS. FOOD STYLING: JOYCE SANGIRARDI

Pork Chops with Rhubarb Chutney

SMART TIPS

✳ **Get a head start.** You can make the chutney up to 2 days in advance; cover and chill. Before serving, warm over low heat (or in the microwave).

✳ **Have it your way.** This piquant chutney is also delicious over chicken.

✳ **Swap fruit.** Don't have currants handy? Use raisins or dried cherries instead.

Prep: 5 min.
Cook: 25 min.
Cool: 30 min.
Serves: 4
Cost per serving:

$2.10

CHUTNEY:
- 2 large stalks rhubarb, trimmed, cut into ½-inch cubes
- ¼ cup cider vinegar
- ¼ tsp. grated orange zest
- 2 Tbsp. currants
- ¼ cup packed light brown sugar
- 1 tsp. minced fresh ginger
- ⅛ tsp. crushed red pepper
- ¼ tsp. salt
- Pinch of ground cloves

PORK:
- 1 Tbsp. olive oil
- 4 ¾-inch-thick boneless pork chops
- Salt and pepper

1 In a saucepan over medium heat, combine rhubarb, vinegar, zest, currants, brown sugar, ginger, crushed red pepper, salt and cloves. Stir in ½ cup water and bring to a simmer. Reduce heat to medium-low and cook, stirring frequently, until rhubarb begins to break down and liquid is almost completely absorbed, about 10 minutes. Transfer to a bowl and let cool to room temperature.

2 Warm oil in a large skillet over medium-high heat. Season chops generously on both sides with salt and pepper. Cook chops, turning once with tongs, until well-browned on both sides and cooked through (an instant-read thermometer inserted in thickest part of chop should read 145°F), about 10 minutes. Serve pork hot, with chutney spooned on top.

PER SERVING: 354 Cal., 14g Fat (4g Sat.), 94mg Chol., 1g Fiber, 38g Pro., 19g Carb., 678mg Sod.

Pea Pancakes with Bacon

Prep: 20 min.
Cook: 15 min.
Serves: 4
Cost per serving:

99¢

- 10 slices bacon
- 1 cup all-purpose flour
- 1 Tbsp. sugar
- 1½ tsp. salt
- 1 tsp. baking powder
- ¼ tsp. baking soda
- 2 Tbsp. chopped chives
- ¾ cup buttermilk, at room temperature
- 2 Tbsp. unsalted butter, melted
- 1½ cups frozen petite peas, defrosted
- 1 large egg, at room temperature

1 On a griddle over medium heat, cook bacon until crisp, 8 to 10 minutes, turning once. Drain on paper towels. Pour off fat; reserve.

2 In a large bowl, whisk together flour, sugar, salt, baking powder, baking soda and chives. In a blender, mix buttermilk, butter and 1 cup peas. Add egg; pulse to combine. Fold buttermilk mixture into dry ingredients until just combined. Fold in remaining ½ cup peas. If batter is too thick, add 1 Tbsp. milk.

3 Warm griddle over medium heat; grease with 2 tsp. reserved bacon fat. In batches, drop ¼ cupfuls of batter onto griddle. Cook until undersides of pancakes are golden, 2 minutes. Flip pancakes with spatula and cook 2 minutes more. Serve pancakes with reserved bacon, sour cream and more chives, if desired.

PER SERVING: 345 Cal., 22g Fat (9g Sat.), 72mg Chol., 2g Fiber, 11g Pro., 25g Carb., 1,084mg Sod.

Baked Ziti with Broccoli and Sausage

Prep: 10 min.
Cook: 35 min.
Serves: 4
Cost per serving:

$1.63

- Salt and pepper
- 8 oz. hot Italian sausage, casings removed
- 2 Tbsp. unsalted butter
- 2 Tbsp. all-purpose flour
- 2 cups milk
- 8 oz. ziti
- 1½ lb. broccoli (about 1 large head), stems removed, florets cut into 1-inch pieces
- ½ cup grated Parmesan

1 Bring a large pot of salted water to a boil over high heat. Preheat oven to 350°F and lightly grease an 11-by-7-inch baking dish. In a large skillet over medium-high heat, cook sausage, stirring and breaking up meat, until no longer pink, about 3 minutes. Add butter and stir well. Sprinkle flour on top and stir for 1 to 2 minutes. Slowly pour in milk and cook, stirring constantly, until smooth and thickened, 3 to 4 minutes. Season sauce with salt and pepper.

2 Add ziti to boiling water and cook until tender, about 5 minutes, then add broccoli and cook for 3 minutes.

Drain ziti and broccoli in a colander and transfer to baking dish. Stir in sausage mixture.

3 Sprinkle Parmesan on top; bake until golden and bubbling, 25 minutes. Serve hot.

PER SERVING: 440 Cal., 22g Fat (5g Sat.), 129mg Chol., 3g Fiber, 50g Pro., 10g Carb., 714mg Sod.

SMART TIP

* Make in advance.
You can prepare this dish up to two days ahead; don't bake. Cover and chill. Bring to room temperature before baking.

SMART TIPS

✳ **Use the best syrup.** Be sure to use 100 percent pure maple syrup, not pancake or maple-flavored syrup. If you can, go with Grade B maple syrup—it has a richer flavor than Grade A (and it's great on pancakes and waffles). Can't find pure maple syrup? Mix 2 tablespoons brown sugar with 1 tablespoon water instead.

✳ **Cook once, eat twice.** Use leftovers to make tasty ham and cheese sandwiches.

Maple-Glazed Ham Steak

Prep: 3 min.

Cook: 12 min.

Serves: 4

Cost per serving:

$2.18

● **1 fully cooked ham steak, about 1¼ lb.**

● **¼ cup maple syrup**
● **2 tsp. Dijon mustard**
● **1 Tbsp. cider vinegar**

1 Preheat broiler to high and set an oven rack about 3 inches from heat source. Line a broiling pan with aluminum foil; mist with cooking spray. Cut ham steak into 4 portions.

2 In a small bowl, stir together maple syrup, mustard and vinegar. Brush one side of ham steak liberally with maple syrup mixture and set on lined broiling pan. Broil ham until glaze is just speckled with golden brown spots and lightly bubbling, about 5 to

7 minutes. Turn and brush other side of ham generously with maple syrup mixture. Broil until glaze is bubbly and speckled with golden brown spots, about 5 minutes longer.
PER SERVING: 244 Cal., 9g Fat (2g Sat.), 101mg Chol., 0g Fiber, 25g Pro., 15g Carb., 1,777mg Sod.

Pork and Hominy Stew

Prep: 25 min.
Cook: 7 hr.
Serves: 8
Cost per serving:

$1.58

- 3 lb. boneless pork shoulder, cut into 2½-inch pieces
- Salt and pepper
- 2 Tbsp. vegetable oil
- 1 onion, chopped
- 2 Tbsp. chili powder
- 3 cloves garlic, finely chopped
- 1 12-oz. bottle beer
- 1 14-oz. can chopped tomatoes with juice
- 3 14-oz. cans white hominy, rinsed and drained
- 1 tsp. dried oregano

1 Sprinkle pork with salt and pepper. Warm oil in a large skillet over medium-high heat. Cook pork, in batches if necessary, browning on all sides, about 10 to 15 minutes. Add pork to slow cooker and drain off all but 1 Tbsp. fat from skillet. Add onion, chili powder and garlic to skillet and cook, stirring frequently, until softened, about 2 minutes. Stir in beer and cook for 1 minute, scraping up browned bits from bottom of pan with a wooden spoon. Add onion mixture to slow cooker.

2 Pour tomatoes with juice over pork and onion mixture in slow cooker. Cover and cook on low until meat is just tender, about 6 hours. Stir in hominy and oregano and cook 1 hour longer. Using tongs, remove pork from slow cooker to a cutting board; let cool slightly.

When pork is cool enough to handle, shred it using your fingers or two forks. Skim fat from top of broth in slow cooker. Return shredded pork to cooker; stir well. Serve hot.

PER SERVING: 391 Cal., 16g Fat (4g Sat.), 111mg Chol., 6g Fiber, 36g Pro., 23g Carb., 1,070mg Sod.

SMART TIP

✳ **Serve with add-ons.** Offer a bowl of chopped cilantro, plus lime wedges and tortilla chips (or crusty rolls) on the side. Toss a salad to go with it.

Honey-Mustard Ham Steaks

Prep: 5 min.
Cook: 10 min.
Serves: 4
Cost per serving:
$2.08

- 2 Tbsp. Dijon mustard
- 2 Tbsp. honey
- 1 Tbsp. light brown sugar
- 1 large (½-inch-thick) precooked ham steak (about 1¼ lb.)
- 8 whole cloves

1 In a small bowl, combine mustard, honey and brown sugar; stir well. If there's a bone in ham steak, remove it. Divide ham steak into 4 equal pieces; spread half of honey-mustard mixture on one side of each and stud each with a clove.

2 Preheat broiler to high and place a rack 2 inches from heat source; line a broiler pan with foil. Put steaks on broiler pan and broil for about 4 minutes. Turn steaks over. Spread remaining mustard mixture over steaks, stud with remaining cloves and broil for about 4 minutes longer, until well browned.

PER SERVING: 211 Cal., 6g Fat (1g Sat.), 75mg Chol., 0g Fiber, 26g Pro., 14g Carb., 1,910mg Sod.

Braised Pork Chops with Apples and Onion

SMART TIPS

✳ Use your oven.
Busy stove? Brown chops in an ovenproof pot, then bake at 325°F for 45 to 50 minutes.

✳ Swap apples.
You can use another type of apple, if you prefer—but make sure it's a hardy baking apple so it doesn't turn to mush. Granny Smith and Rome work well.

✳ Create balance.
A baked potato and a steamed green vegetable round out the meal.

Prep: 5 min.
Cook: 40 min.
Serves: 4
Cost per serving:

$2.43

- 4 ½-inch-thick bone-in pork chops, 4 to 6 oz. each
- Salt and pepper

- 2 Tbsp. unsalted butter
- 2 Tbsp. vegetable oil
- 1 onion, thinly sliced
- 1 cup low-sodium chicken broth
- 3 Golden Delicious apples, peeled, cored and chopped
- 2 Tbsp. chopped fresh parsley, optional

1 Pat chops dry and season on both sides with salt and pepper.

2 Melt butter with oil in a large pot over medium-high heat. Add chops and cook until lightly browned, about 5 minutes per side. Remove to a plate; pour off all but 1 Tbsp. fat from pot. Add onion and cook, stirring, until softened slightly, about 3 minutes. Pour in broth, increase heat to high and stir to remove any browned bits from bottom.

3 Return chops to pot; add apples. Reduce heat to medium, cover pot and cook until chops are tender and apples are softened, about 30 minutes. Serve chops topped with apples, onion and parsley, if desired.

PER SERVING: 410 Cal., 26g Fat (9g Sat), 88mg Chol., 2g Fiber, 28g Pro., 17g Carb., 961mg Sod.

Soy-Marinated Pork Chops

Prep: 5 min.
Cook: 7 min.
Serves: 4
Cost per serving:

$2.18

- 4 boneless center-cut pork chops (about 6 oz. each), pounded to ½-inch thickness
- ¼ cup soy sauce
- 2 Tbsp. rice wine vinegar
- 2 tsp. sesame oil
- 1 Tbsp. chopped fresh cilantro
- 3 scallions, white and light green parts, chopped

1 Place pork chops, soy sauce, vinegar and oil in a large ziplock bag; seal. Turn bag several times to coat chops with marinade; place in refrigerator for 15 minutes.

2 Remove pork chops from bag; discard excess marinade. Warm a grill or grill pan to medium-high heat. Grill pork chops until cooked through, about 3½ minutes per side. Transfer to a platter, sprinkle with cilantro and scallions, and serve.

PER SERVING: 321 Cal., 19g Fat (7g Sat.), 89mg Chol., 0g Fiber, 33g Pro., 5g Carb., 1,547mg Sod.

SMART TIPS

✳ **Choose sides.** These Asian-flavored chops go especially well with rice (either white or brown) and steamed snow peas. Alternatively, heat up a bag of frozen Asian-style mixed vegetables.

✳ **Keep leftovers.** If you have extra pork, wrap it tightly in plastic or foil and refrigerate. Cut it into pieces and add it to a quick stir-fry for dinner on another night.

✳ **Go easy.** Sesame oil adds a lot of nutty flavor to dishes, but be sure to use it sparingly. Its strong taste can overpower a dish if you use too much. Try it in marinades, or drizzle it on at the end of cooking time.

✳ **Use the right vinegar.** Rice wine vinegar is available in the Asian or ethnic foods section of many supermarkets. If you can't find it (or don't care for it), swap in cider vinegar and add a pinch of sugar.

CHOP HERBS WITH EASE

Adding a handful of fresh herbs can make your meals sparkle. Follow these simple steps and you'll be prepping like a pro.

1 **Rinse them off.** Dry herbs are easiest to chop. Wash them in cool running water, then use paper towels to pat them dry gently but thoroughly.

2 **Strip them down.** If you're chopping an herb that has a woody stem, such as thyme or rosemary, remove the leaves with your fingers and discard the stem. For herbs with softer stems, like parsley or tarragon, chop off the lower stems and keep the leafy upper parts.

3 **Chop them up.** Once you've removed the stems, pile the herbs in the center of your cutting board. Using the heel of a sharp chef's knife, give them a rough chop, then re-pile and chop again. Using a rocking motion, raise the knife handle up and down quickly, always leaving the tip of the knife on the cutting board so it acts as a hinge. Be careful not to overchop or the herbs will blacken.

Chili-Lime Pork Tenderloin

Prep: 8 min.
Cook: 27 min.
Serves: 6
Cost per serving:

$1.56

- 1½ lb. pork tenderloin
- Salt and pepper
- 1 tsp. chili powder
- 1 Tbsp. fresh lime juice
- 1 tsp. soy sauce
- ½ tsp. sugar
- 2 Tbsp. vegetable oil

1 Preheat oven to 400°F. Line a large rimmed baking sheet with foil. Pat pork dry and season on all sides with salt and pepper.

2 Mix chili powder with lime juice, soy sauce and sugar. Rub mixture into pork. Warm a large skillet over high heat; add oil. Sear pork on all sides, turning with tongs, about 2 minutes. Place skillet in oven; roast until a thermometer inserted in center of tenderloin reads 145°F, 20 to 25 minutes, depending on thickness. While roasting, baste pork with any juices that have accumulated. Add water, 2 Tbsp. at a time, if needed, to prevent scorching.

3 Remove tenderloin to a cutting board, cover loosely with foil and let sit for 5 minutes. Slice on diagonal into ½-inch-thick pieces and serve.

PER SERVING: 182 Cal., 9g Fat (2g Sat.), 74mg Chol., 0g Fiber, 24g Pro., 1g Carb., 305mg Sod.

Tortellini with Ham and Peas

SMART TIPS

❋ **Watch out.** Take care not to overcook the tortellini—it's OK if the pasta is still a little firm, as it will cook an additional 2 to 3 minutes in the sauce. You don't want it to become mushy.

❋ **Keep your cool.** There's no need to defrost the peas—just throw them in the pot with the tortellini (to heat them through) 30 seconds before draining.

❋ **Swap the veggies.** If you don't care for peas, or you have another type of frozen vegetable on hand, make the switch. This dish is also delicious with broccoli florets, asparagus tips, sliced carrots or a vegetable mixture.

Prep: 5 min.
Cook: 10 min.
Serves: 6
Cost per serving:

$1.05

- Salt and pepper
- 1 lb. fresh or frozen cheese tortellini

- 1 cup frozen peas
- 3 Tbsp. unsalted butter, cut into small pieces
- ½ cup heavy cream
- ½ cup grated Parmesan
- ¼ lb. ham, chopped

1 Bring a large pot of salted water to boil over high heat. Stir in tortellini and cook until pasta is just al dente (do not overcook), as package label directs. Add peas to pot for final 30 seconds to 1 minute of cooking time.

2 Drain tortellini and peas in a colander and immediately return to pot. Stir in butter, cream, Parmesan and ham. Season with salt and pepper. Turn stove on to medium heat and cook tortellini mixture, stirring frequently, until butter has melted, ingredients are heated through and sauce has thickened slightly, about 2 to 3 minutes. Serve immediately.

PER SERVING: 420 Cal., 21g Fat (12g Sat.), 96mg Chol., 4g Fiber, 19g Pro., 39g Carb., 896mg Sod.

CHARLES SCHILLER; FOOD STYLING: LYNN MILLER

SMART TIPS

✳ **Serve it up.** For a different take on this dish, offer the cutlets on sandwich rolls with tomato sauce and melted mozzarella.

✳ **Save on ingredients.** Waste less, spend less and eat more healthfully by making your own bread crumbs. Store heels of loaves and extra slices in the freezer. Lightly toast bread, then grind in a food processor.

✳ **Cook with chicken.** You can make this dish with boneless, skinless chicken breast halves. Pound them into cutlets with a meat mallet and follow the recipe.

Parmesan Pork Cutlets

Prep: 10 min.
Cook: 15 min.
Serves: 4
Cost per serving:

$1.51

- ½ cup all-purpose flour
- 2 large eggs
- ½ cup grated Parmesan
- ¾ cup plain bread crumbs
- 1 lb. boneless pork cutlets (4 cutlets)
- Salt and pepper
- 2 Tbsp. vegetable oil
- 2 Tbsp. unsalted butter

1 Place flour in a shallow bowl. Whisk eggs together in a separate shallow bowl. Combine Parmesan and bread crumbs in a third shallow bowl.

2 Sprinkle cutlets with salt and pepper. One at a time, dredge cutlets in flour, dip in egg and coat with bread crumb mixture.

3 Warm 1 Tbsp. oil and 1 Tbsp. butter in a large skillet over medium heat until butter is foaming. Cook half of cutlets, turning once, until browned on both sides and cooked through, about 5 minutes total. Transfer to platter and loosely cover with foil to keep warm; repeat process with remaining oil, butter and dredged cutlets. Serve immediately.

PER SERVING: 479 Cal., 24g Fat (9g Sat.), 201mg Chol., 1g Fiber, 36g Pro., 27g Carb., 725mg Sod.

Monte Cristo Sandwiches

Prep: 5 min.
Cook: 12 min.
Serves: 4
Cost per serving:
$1.82

- **2 large eggs**
- **½ cup milk**
- **8 slices sturdy white sandwich bread**
- **4 slices turkey breast**
- **4 slices Swiss cheese**
- **4 slices Black Forest or other ham**
- **1 Tbsp. unsalted butter**
- **Confectioners' sugar (optional)**
- **¼ cup raspberry or strawberry jam (optional)**

1 In a wide, shallow bowl, whisk together eggs and milk to combine. Lay a slice of bread on a work surface and top with 1 slice turkey, 1 slice cheese, 1 slice ham and a second slice of bread. Repeat to assemble remaining sandwiches.

2 Warm a large nonstick frying pan over medium-high heat. Melt butter (if pan is not large enough to accommodate all 4 sandwiches, melt half of butter and cook sandwiches in 2 batches). When butter foams, swirl pan to coat. Carefully dip each sandwich in egg mixture, turning to lightly coat both sides, and lay sandwiches in hot pan. Cook, flipping over once with a spatula, until sandwiches are well-browned on both sides, 4 to 6 minutes total.

3 To serve, cut sandwiches in half diagonally and sprinkle lightly with confectioners' sugar, if desired. Top each sandwich half with a small dollop of jam, or serve jam alongside for dipping.

PER SERVING: 414 Cal., 18g Fat (9g Sat.), 169mg Chol., 1g Fiber, 26g Pro., 36g Carb., 989mg Sod.

SMART TIP

* **Shake it off.** Be sure to get as much egg mixture off the sandwiches as possible before cooking—leaving too much on will make them soggy.

CHARLES SCHILLER; FOOD STYLING: LYNN MILLER

Penne with Sweet Peas and Prosciutto

Prep: 10 min.
Cook: 15 min.
Serves: 6
Cost per serving:

$1.52

- Salt
- 1 lb. penne pasta
- 1 Tbsp. olive oil
- 6 Tbsp. unsalted butter
- 1 onion, chopped
- 4 oz. thinly sliced prosciutto, halved lengthwise and cut into ½-inch strips
- 1 10-oz. package frozen peas, thawed
- 1 cup grated Parmesan, plus more for serving
- ¼ tsp. pepper
- 1 tsp. grated lemon zest

1 In a large pot of boiling salted water, cook pasta until al dente, about 12 minutes. Drain and return to pot. Toss with oil.

2 While pasta is cooking, melt 1 Tbsp. butter in a large nonstick skillet over medium heat. Add onion and cook, stirring, until translucent, 5 minutes. Add prosciutto and sauté for 2 minutes. Add peas and sauté for 3 minutes.

3 Toss mixture with pasta in pot, along with remaining 5 Tbsp. butter, Parmesan, 1 tsp. salt, pepper and lemon zest. Heat through.

4 Serve pasta with more cheese if desired.
PER SERVING: 541 Cal., 24g Fat (Sat. 13g), 55mg Chol., 10g Fiber, 25g Pro., 54g Carb., 1,142mg Sod.

SMART TIPS
✳ **Ham it up.** Buy prosciutto, an air-cured ham imported from Italy, in packages at the market or sliced to order at the deli counter. You also can substitute regular bacon, but cook it first.

✳ **Go green.** Stir cooked spinach into this dish for a shot of color and nutrients.

Salami and Swiss Hoagies

Prep: 10 min.
Serves: 4
Cost per serving:

$2.01

- 4 Italian sandwich rolls
- ¼ cup reduced-fat mayonnaise
- 2 Tbsp. olive oil
- 1 tsp. red wine vinegar
- 1 tsp. dried oregano
- 2 cups shredded green-leaf lettuce
- ½ small red onion, thinly sliced
- 4 oz. hard salami, thinly sliced
- 4 oz. Swiss cheese, thinly sliced
- Salt and pepper

1 Using a serrated knife, slice sandwich rolls lengthwise without cutting all the way through. Spread both sides of each roll with 1 Tbsp. mayonnaise.

2 Whisk olive oil, vinegar and oregano together in a large bowl. Add lettuce and onion and toss with vinaigrette until lightly coated.

3 Layer one side of rolls, alternating ¼ each of salami and cheese slices. Top with dressed lettuce and onion. Season with salt and pepper. Fold sandwiches closed and secure with toothpicks.
PER SERVING: 527 Cal., 30g Fat (10g Sat.), 56mg Chol., 1g Fiber, 22g Pro., 43g Carb., 1,360mg Sod.

SMART TIP
✳ **Choose a side.** Offer baby carrots or celery with the hoagies.

Ham and Cheddar Supper Waffles

SMART TIPS

* **Top it off.** Serve these waffles with a drizzle of maple syrup or with tomato salsa.

* **Enjoy in the a.m.** This dish makes a fun supper, but it's also ideal for a weekend breakfast or brunch.

* **Make them hearty.** Swap in half whole-wheat flour to boost the nutrients and fiber, and to lend a nuttier flavor.

* **Cook extras.** Waffles freeze well, so make more than you need, wrap them in plastic, place them in a heavy-duty ziplock bag and freeze.

Prep: 10 min.
Cook: 10 min. per waffle
Serves: 4
Cost per serving:

92¢

- 1½ cups all-purpose flour
- 1½ tsp. baking powder
- 1 tsp. sugar
- ¼ tsp. salt
- 1½ cups milk
- 1 large egg, lightly beaten
- 4 Tbsp. unsalted butter, melted and cooled
- 2 oz. thinly sliced ham, chopped
- 1 cup shredded sharp Cheddar

1 Preheat oven to 200°F; line a baking sheet with foil. Heat waffle iron. Whisk together flour, baking powder, sugar and salt in a large mixing bowl. Stir milk, egg and butter into flour mixture until just combined. Fold in ham and cheese.

2 Mist waffle iron with nonstick cooking spray. Pour about ¾ cup batter onto waffle iron and carefully spread to edges with a spatula. Cook until waffles are golden, 8 to 10 minutes. Place cooked waffles on baking sheet; keep warm in oven. Repeat with remaining batter, misting waffle iron with cooking spray as needed between batches. Serve immediately.

PER SERVING (1 waffle): 509 Cal., 28g Fat (17g Sat.), 140mg Chol., 1g Fiber, 21g Pro., 42g Carb., 676mg Sod.

Barbecued-Pork Sliders

Prep: 20 min.
Chill: 8 hr.
Cook: 5 hr. 45 min.
Yield: 24
Cost per serving:

$1.98

- 1 4-lb. shoulder pork roast
- 24 small dinner rolls

SPICE RUB:
- 1 Tbsp. paprika
- 1 Tbsp. garlic powder
- 1 Tbsp. packed dark brown sugar
- 1 Tbsp. dry mustard
- 1 Tbsp. onion powder
- 1 tsp. dried thyme
- 1 tsp. dried oregano
- Salt and pepper
- ½ tsp. cayenne pepper

SAUCE MIX:
- 2 onions, chopped
- 1 green bell pepper, seeded and chopped
- ½ cup packed dark brown sugar
- ¼ cup cider vinegar
- 1 6-oz. can tomato paste
- 1½ Tbsp. chili powder
- 1 tsp. dried mustard
- 3 tsp. Worcestershire sauce
- 1 tsp. salt

PICKLED ONION:
- 1 Tbsp. sugar
- 1 tsp. salt
- ½ cup white vinegar
- 1 red onion, thinly sliced

1 Remove skin and excess fat from pork. Combine all spice-rub ingredients and rub all over meat. Place pork on a large plate, cover with plastic wrap and refrigerate for 8 hours or overnight.

2 Combine all sauce-mix ingredients in slow cooker, place pork on top, cover and cook on high until meat is tender and can be shredded easily with a fork, about 5½ hours.

3 Make pickled onion: Stir sugar and salt into vinegar until dissolved; stir in onion. Cover and refrigerate for 2 to 3 hours, stirring occasionally.

4 Remove pork from slow cooker. Remove 2 cups of sauce. Shred meat. Stir pork back into slow cooker, cover and cook for 15 minutes.

5 Split rolls, top with meat and pickled onion. Serve, passing reserved sauce separately.

PER SERVING (3 SLIDERS):
612 Cal., 18g Fat (6g Sat.), 88mg Chol., 5g Fiber, 53g Pro., 58g Carb., 770mg Sod.

JOHN MONTANA. FOOD STYLING: LYNN MILLER

Fried Rice with Ham and Asparagus

Prep: 5 min.
Cook: 11 min.
Serves: 4
Cost per serving:

$1.79

- Salt
- 1 lb. asparagus, trimmed and cut into 1-inch pieces
- 3 Tbsp. vegetable oil
- 3 large eggs, lightly beaten
- 5 oz. thick-sliced deli ham, cut into ¼-inch pieces
- 2 cloves garlic, finely chopped
- 4 cups cold cooked white rice
- 3 Tbsp. soy sauce
- 5 scallions, finely chopped

1 Bring a medium saucepan of salted water to boil. Add asparagus; cook until just tender, 2 minutes. Drain; set aside.

2 Warm 1 Tbsp. vegetable oil in a large skillet over medium-high heat. Add eggs and cook without stirring until set around the edges, about 30 seconds. Break eggs into pieces with a spatula and stir until fully cooked and set, about 1 minute longer. Scrape eggs into a bowl.

3 Warm remaining 2 Tbsp. vegetable oil in skillet. Add ham and garlic and cook, stirring frequently, until garlic is fragrant. Add rice and soy sauce and cook, stirring, until rice is coated with sauce and very hot, 3 to 4 minutes. Stir in reserved asparagus and eggs and cook for another minute, stirring. Toss in scallions; cook for 1 minute longer, stirring constantly. Serve immediately.

PER SERVING: 452 Cal., 18g Fat (3g Sat.), 180mg Chol., 4g Fiber, 20g Pro., 53g Carb., 837mg Sod.

SMART TIP

✳ **Make it faster.**
Cold rice works best for this recipe. If you don't have cold leftover rice, cook some in the morning.

RYAN BENYI, FOOD STYLING: STEPHANA BOTTOM

SMART TIPS

❋ **Try another variety.** Exchange the Gruyère for a cheese of your choice. Cheddar, fontina and Swiss are all delicious in this recipe.

❋ **Make it a meal.** Mashed sweet potatoes are a great side with this dish—the sweetness complements the saltiness of the pork and the cheese. Baked sweet potatoes also work well. Or, for an autumn treat, try roasted butternut or acorn squash as an accompaniment.

Stuffed Smoked Pork Chops

Prep: 5 min.

Cook: 9 min.

Serves: 4

Cost per serving:

$2.25

- 4 ½-inch-thick, bone-in smoked pork chops
- 1 cup grated Gruyère
- 1 Tbsp. Dijon mustard
- Pepper
- 2 Tbsp. vegetable oil

1 Using a sharp paring knife, cut through the middle of each pork chop to the bone to make a pocket.

2 Combine Gruyère and mustard in a bowl. Divide cheese mixture and spoon into each pocket, pressing down to flatten chop. Sprinkle chops with pepper.

3 Warm oil in a large skillet over medium-high heat. Cook chops, turning once, until browned on each side, about 3 to 4 minutes per side. Remove from heat, cover pan and let stand until cheese has melted, 4 to 5 minutes.

PER SERVING: 366 Cal., 27g Fat (10g Sat.), 89mg Chol., 0g Fiber, 30g Pro., 2g Carb., 541mg Sod.

Cider-Braised Pork Medallions

Prep: 5 min.
Cook: 18 min.
Serves: 4
Cost per serving:

$1.19

- 1 pork tenderloin (about 1¼ lb.)
- ¼ cup all-purpose flour
- Salt and pepper
- 2 Tbsp. unsalted butter
- 2 Tbsp. vegetable oil
- ¾ cup low-sodium chicken broth
- ¾ cup apple cider

1 Cut pork into 8 1¼-inch-thick medallions. In a bowl, mix flour, ½ tsp. salt and ¼ tsp. pepper. Dredge pork in flour mixture and shake off any excess.

2 In a large skillet over medium-high heat, warm butter and oil until butter melts. Cook pork, in batches if necessary, until lightly browned, about 4 minutes per side. Remove to a plate; cover with foil to keep warm.

3 Pour off any fat remaining in skillet. Return skillet to heat and pour in broth and cider. Increase heat to high and bring to a boil. Boil rapidly, stirring with a wooden spoon to pick up browned bits on bottom of skillet, until liquid is reduced by half, about 5 minutes.

4 Return pork to skillet, reduce heat to medium and cook, turning, until sauce is syrupy and pork is cooked through, about 5 minutes.

PER SERVING: 338 Cal., 18g Fat (6g Sat.), 107mg Chol., 0g Fiber, 31g Pro., 12g Carb., 467mg Sod.

SMART TIPS

❋ **Try poultry.** This dish is also delicious with the same amount of skinless, boneless chicken breasts. Rinse the chicken, pat dry and slice into strips.

❋ **Choose juice instead.** Can't find apple cider? Substitute apple juice. Just be sure to look for a variety that is 100 percent juice.

Three-Bean Chili with Bacon

Prep: 5 min.
Cook: 25 min.
Serves: 4
Cost per serving:

$1.98

- 2 slices bacon, cut into ¼-inch pieces
- 1 onion, finely chopped
- 2 cloves garlic, finely chopped
- ¼ cup chili powder
- 1 15-oz. can white beans, drained and rinsed
- 1 15-oz. can kidney beans, drained and rinsed
- 1 15-oz. can black beans, drained and rinsed
- 1 28-oz. can diced tomatoes
- 1 cup low-sodium chicken broth
- Salt

1 Cook bacon in a skillet over medium heat until softened but not crispy, about 2 minutes. Drain all but 1 Tbsp. fat from skillet. Add onion and garlic and cook over medium-high heat, stirring, until onion has softened, about 3 minutes. Stir in chili powder and cook, stirring, for 30 seconds.

2 Stir in beans, tomatoes and broth and bring briefly to a boil. Turn heat to medium-low and simmer until chili is slightly thickened, about 15 minutes. Season with salt and serve.

PER SERVING: 380 Cal., 5g Fat (1g Sat.), 8mg Chol., 19g Fiber, 23g Pro., 69g Carb., 1,999mg Sod.

Molasses-and-Mustard-Glazed Ribs

RYAN BENYI; FOOD STYLING: STEPHANA BOTTOM

Prep: 15 min.
Cook: 6 hr.
Serves: 6
Cost per serving:
$1.71

- ½ cup Dijon mustard
- ½ cup dark (not blackstrap) molasses
- ¼ cup packed light brown sugar
- 2 Tbsp. tomato paste
- ¼ cup cider vinegar
- 1 tsp. salt
- ½ tsp. garlic powder
- ¼ tsp. cayenne pepper
- 4 lb. country-style pork ribs or baby back ribs, cut into 4-rib sections

1 Combine mustard, molasses, sugar, tomato paste, vinegar, salt, garlic powder and cayenne pepper in a small saucepan. Bring to a boil, lower heat and simmer until thickened, about 5 minutes. Set aside to cool.

2 Brush rib sections thickly with sauce and arrange in slow cooker. Cover and cook on low until meat is tender and easily removed from bone, 4 to 6 hours. Skim fat from sauce and spoon sauce over ribs before serving.

PER SERVING: 618 Cal., 25g Fat (9g Sat.), 194mg Chol., 0g Fiber, 59g Pro., 31g Carb., 1,090mg Sod.

White Bean Soup

SMART TIPS

❋ Switch beans. White beans such as cannellini are especially tasty in this hearty soup. But you can use any variety of bean you like, or a combination.

❋ Dress it up. For extra color, sprinkle the soup with additional chopped thyme just before serving. Offer a green salad and crusty rolls on the side to make the soup a complete meal.

CHARLES SCHILLER; FOOD STYLING: LYNN MILLER

Prep: 10 min.
Cook: 5 hr.
Serves: 6
Cost per serving:

$1.05

- 2 Tbsp. olive oil
- 1 small onion, finely chopped
- 3 cloves garlic, finely chopped

- 3 15.5-oz. cans white beans, rinsed and drained
- 1 smoked pork chop or 2 smoked ham hocks
- 2 cups low-sodium chicken broth
- 3 sprigs fresh thyme
- Salt and pepper

1 Warm olive oil in a large skillet over medium heat. Add onion and cook, stirring occasionally, until onion is softened, about 5 minutes. Add garlic and cook until fragrant, 1 minute more.

2 Scrape onions and garlic into a slow cooker. Add beans, pork chop, broth, 1 cup water and thyme, cover and cook on low heat for 4 to 5 hours, until beans are tender and flavors have blended and developed, adding more water during cooking if necessary.

3 Remove and discard thyme sprigs. Remove pork chop and shred meat. Stir shredded meat back into soup. Season soup with salt and pepper, and serve hot.

PER SERVING: 513 Cal., 18g Fat (5g Sat.), 61mg Chol., 11g Fiber, 38g Pro., 51g Carb., 657mg Sod.

Apricot-Onion Pork Medallions

Prep: 5 min.
Cook: 16 min.
Serves: 4
Cost per serving:

$1.97

- 1 lb. pork tenderloin, cut into 1-inch slices
- ½ tsp. dried thyme
- ½ tsp. salt
- 2 Tbsp. olive oil
- 1 Tbsp. unsalted butter
- 1 onion, thinly sliced
- ½ cup low-sodium chicken broth
- 2 Tbsp. apricot jam
- 1 Tbsp. Dijon mustard

1 Flatten each pork slice to ¾ inch by placing it between 2 sheets of plastic wrap and pounding it with a meat mallet or rolling pin. Sprinkle both sides of pork with thyme and salt. Warm olive oil over medium-high heat in a large heavy skillet. Cook medallions, turning once, until well browned on both sides, about 3 minutes total. (Work in batches if skillet is too small to fit all of pork at once.) Transfer to a plate.

2 Add butter to pan and allow to melt. Add onion and cook, stirring occasionally, until softened, about

3 minutes. Add broth, jam and mustard and bring to a boil, stirring. Cover skillet, lower heat and simmer sauce until onion is very soft, about 5 minutes.

3 Return pork medallions to skillet, turning with tongs to coat with sauce. Cover

skillet and simmer until pork is cooked through, about 5 minutes longer. Transfer pork to a platter, spoon sauce over and serve immediately.
PER SERVING: 269 Cal., 14g Fat (4g Sat.), 83mg Chol., 1g Fiber, 25g Pro., 10g Carb., 478mg Sod.

SMART TIP

✳ **Round out the dish.** To make this a satisfying meal, serve with mashed potatoes and broccoli, green beans or zucchini.

MARK THOMAS. FOOD STYLING: LYNN MILLER

SMART TIPS

✳ **Go south of the border.** Spice up this chowder by adding 4 ounces chopped green chilies, 2 teaspoons chili powder and 1 teaspoon cumin. Sprinkle individual bowls with chopped fresh cilantro.

✳ **Lower the fat.** For a lighter version of this soup, use whole milk instead of half-and-half and swap in turkey bacon instead of regular.

Creamy Corn Chowder

Prep: 15 min.
Cook: 30 min.
Serves: 8
Cost per serving:

$1.38

- 6 slices bacon, cut into 1-inch pieces
- 1 medium onion, chopped
- 2 stalks celery, chopped
- 1 medium red bell pepper, seeded and chopped
- 3 medium red potatoes, diced
- 1 1-lb. bag frozen corn kernels, thawed
- 1 tsp. dried thyme
- Salt and pepper
- ⅓ cup all-purpose flour
- 6 cups chicken broth
- 1 bay leaf
- 1 cup half-and-half

1 In a 4-quart soup pot, cook bacon over medium-high heat, stirring frequently, until brown and crispy, about 5 minutes. Pour off all but 2 Tbsp. fat.

2 Add onion, celery and bell pepper and cook, stirring, until vegetables have softened, 4 to 5 minutes. Add potatoes, corn, thyme, salt and pepper. Stir to combine.

3 Sprinkle flour over mixture and stir until thickened and fragrant, about 3 minutes.

4 Slowly pour in broth, stirring constantly until smooth. Add bay leaf; bring to a boil. Reduce heat; simmer until potatoes are tender, 25 minutes.

5 Remove bay leaf and stir in half-and-half. Cook until warmed through. Serve hot.

PER SERVING: 213 Cal., 12g Fat, (5g Sat.), 18mg Chol., 4g Fiber, 7g Pro., 22g Carb., 1,472mg Sod.

Western Frittata

Prep: 5 min.
Cook: 15 min.
Serves: 4
Cost per serving:

$1.25

- 2 Tbsp. vegetable oil
- 1 small onion, chopped
- ½ green bell pepper, seeded and diced
- 6 oz. boiled ham, diced
- 8 large eggs
- Salt and pepper
- ½ cup shredded Cheddar

1 Preheat broiler; set rack about 6 inches from heat source.

2 Warm oil in a large, ovenproof nonstick skillet over medium-high heat. Add onion and pepper and cook, stirring, until softened, about 3 minutes. Stir in ham and sauté 1 minute.

3 Whisk eggs with salt and pepper until smooth and blended. Pour evenly over vegetable mixture in skillet. Place skillet over medium-low heat and cook, shaking often, until frittata is almost set in center and lightly browned on bottom, 10 to 12 minutes. Sprinkle cheese over top.

4 Transfer skillet to broiler and cook, watching carefully to avoid burning, until cheese is bubbly, 1 to 2 minutes. Cut into wedges and serve hot or at room temperature. **PER SERVING:** 337 Cal., 24g Fat (7g Sat.), 460mg Chol., 1g Fiber, 26g Pro., 4g Carb., 1,171mg Sod.

SMART TIPS

✳ **Cook evenly.** The frittata will start to set after about 3 minutes on the stove. Run a long spatula under it to loosen it—that will make it easier to shake the pan and ensure even cooking.

✳ **Add a bit of green...or take some out.** Swap in scallions for the onion to add a boost of color. Green peppers are traditional in a Western omelet, but you can use red if you prefer them.

✳ **Let it cool.** You can make this frittata in advance and serve it at room temperature, on its own or in a sandwich. It also makes a delicious brunch dish.

✳ **Switch cheeses.** Try grated Parmesan or shredded Swiss in place of the Cheddar.

KEEP CAST IRON IN TIP-TOP SHAPE

Follow a few steps to season your pan, and your cookware will last a lifetime.

1 **Give it a rinse.** If you're seasoning a brand-new pan, wash it with a stiff brush and hot soapy water. Then rinse and dry completely.

2 **Oil it up.** Using a brush or paper towel, evenly coat the pan with a thin layer (about 1 tablespoon) of a neutral oil, such as corn or grapeseed, or melted vegetable shortening.

3 **Bake it.** Preheat oven to 350°F. Place your pan upside down on a foil-lined baking sheet and put it on the oven's middle rack. Bake for one hour. Turn off the oven and let the pan cool completely before removing.

Bacon-and-Pea-Stuffed Potatoes

Prep: 10 min.
Cook: 25 min.
Serves: 4
Cost per serving:

$2.21

- 4 6-oz. baking potatoes
- 2 Tbsp. unsalted butter
- Salt and pepper
- ½ cup milk
- ½ lb. bacon, cooked until crisp, crumbled
- 1½ cups frozen peas, thawed (6 oz.)
- 2 cups grated Cheddar (8 oz.)

1 Preheat oven to 450°F. Scrub potatoes, dry well and pierce several times with a fork. Microwave for 4 minutes on high. Turn potatoes over and cook for 4 more minutes. Turn again, cook on low for 2 minutes, turn and cook another 2 minutes. Transfer potatoes to a work surface and cover with a bowl. Let sit for 5 minutes.

2 Slice a ¼-inch "lid" off top of each potato; discard. With a small spoon, scoop out flesh, leaving a shell with a ¼-inch "wall" of flesh.

3 Mix scooped-out potato with butter, salt, pepper and milk in a large bowl. Mash with a fork until blended (mixture should be chunky). Stir in bacon, peas and 1 cup cheese. Fill potato skins with equal amounts of potato mixture. Top with remaining cheese and bake until cheese has melted and filling is warmed, about 10 minutes.

PER SERVING: 671 Cal., 43g Fat (24g Sat.), 131mg Chol., 6g Fiber, 37g Pro., 34g Carb., 1,840mg Sod.

Spinach Salad with Chickpeas and Warm Bacon Vinaigrette

Prep: 5 min.

Cook: 12 min.

Serves: 4

Cost per serving:

$1.24

- 6 slices bacon
- 1 15-oz. can chickpeas, rinsed, drained and patted dry
- 8 oz. spinach, stems removed
- 2 Tbsp. cider vinegar
- 1 Tbsp. Dijon mustard
- 1 Tbsp. olive oil
- 8 dried figs, stemmed and sliced
- ¼ cup crumbled blue cheese, optional

1 Cook bacon in a large skillet over medium-high heat until crisp, about 5 minutes. Pour off all but 1 Tbsp. bacon fat; reserve fat (you should have about 1 Tbsp. left). Place bacon on paper towels to drain; when cool enough to handle, use your hands to crumble.

2 Add chickpeas to same skillet and cook, stirring constantly, until they are lightly browned and slightly crisped, 7 to 10 minutes. Place spinach in a large salad bowl; scatter chickpeas over spinach.

3 Remove skillet from heat and carefully whisk in cider vinegar (watch out, as mixture can splatter). Stir in mustard and, while skillet is still warm, vigorously whisk in reserved bacon fat and olive oil. Quickly pour dressing into bowl with spinach. Add figs and crumbled bacon and toss well, until all of spinach is dressed.

4 Sprinkle with cheese, if using, and serve immediately.

PER SERVING: 279 Cal., 13g Fat (5g Sat.), 29mg Chol., 6g Fiber, 14g Pro., 28g Carb., 926mg Sod.

SMART TIP

❋ **Dish it out.** This salad is hearty enough to enjoy as a main course, or it will serve 6 to 8 as an appetizer.

RYAN BENYI, FOOD STYLING: ANDREA STEINBERG

Pasta Carbonara Frittata

Prep: 5 min.
Cook: 25 min.
Serves: 4
Cost per serving:

$1.52

- Salt and pepper
- 8 oz. spaghetti
- 2 Tbsp. olive oil
- 4 oz. bacon
- 6 large eggs
- ½ cup grated Parmesan
- 2 cloves garlic, finely chopped

1 Bring a large pot of salted water to boil and cook spaghetti until just tender, about 8 minutes, or as package label directs. Drain, transfer to a large bowl and toss with olive oil to coat. Let cool to room temperature.

2 Cook bacon in a large skillet over medium-high heat until crisp, 5 to 8 minutes. Remove bacon to paper towels to drain. Discard all but 1 Tbsp. of fat in skillet.

3 Preheat broiler to high. Whisk together eggs, Parmesan, garlic, ½ tsp. salt and ¼ tsp. pepper in a bowl. Pour over spaghetti and toss to coat. Crumble bacon into bowl and mix well.

4 Place skillet back on stove over medium-low heat and carefully pour in egg-and-spaghetti mixture, spreading it into an even layer with a spatula. Cook until bottom is well-browned, about 8 minutes, sliding a spatula underneath frittata occasionally to loosen from skillet.

5 Place skillet under broiler and cook until top of frittata is golden and set, about 3 minutes. Let stand for 5 minutes, then cut into wedges and serve.
PER SERVING: 387 Cal., 23g Fat (8g Sat.), 359mg Chol., 1g Fiber, 22g Pro., 19g Carb., 663mg Sod.

SMART TIP

✳ **Mix it up.** To vary this dish, swap sausage or pepperoni for the bacon, or add sun-dried tomatoes or cooked broccoli florets.

SMART TIPS

✳ **Swap the beans.** Try navy beans, red kidney beans or black-eyed peas—or a mixture—instead of black beans.

✳ **Dress it up.** Add a cup of yellow corn, a small can of diced chilies or chopped jarred pimientos just before the end of the cooking time for extra color and flavor, or sprinkle in a few drops of hot sauce.

✳ **Use up leftovers.** Instead of sausage, stir in cut-up leftover ham, chicken or beef. Or try chicken or turkey sausage.

Black Bean Soup with Sausage

Prep: 5 min.
Cook: 6 hr.
Serves: 6
Cost per serving:

$1.53

- 2 tsp. olive oil
- 1 onion, diced
- 3 cloves garlic, chopped
- 1 16-oz. jar salsa
- 2 15.5-oz. cans black beans
- 1 cup low-sodium chicken broth
- 2 3-oz. hot Italian sausage links
- ½ cup chopped cilantro
- Salt and pepper

1 Warm oil in a medium skillet over medium heat. Add onion and garlic and cook, stirring frequently, until onion is softened and translucent, about 5 minutes.

2 Combine onion mixture, beans (with their liquid), salsa and broth in a slow cooker. Stir well, cover and cook on low for 5 hours.

3 Stir sausages into bean mixture in slow cooker and cook for 1 hour longer.

4 Using tongs, remove sausages to a cutting board; cut into bite-size pieces with a sharp knife. Return sausages to slow cooker. Stir in cilantro and season with salt and pepper. Serve soup hot in bowls, with chopped avocado on top and sour cream on the side, if desired.

PER SERVING: 635 Cal., 11g Fat (3g Sat.), 21mg Chol., 29g Fiber, 38g Pro., 101g Carb., 1,025mg Sod.

CHARLES SCHILLER; FOOD STYLING: LYNN MILLER

RYAN BENYI
FOOD STYLING:

Ham, Swiss and Spinach Quiche

Prep: 10 min.
Bake: 40 min.
Serves: 8
Cost per serving:

$1.20

- 3 cups packed baby spinach, chopped
- 6 large eggs, lightly beaten
- 1½ cups half-and-half
- ½ tsp. salt
- 1 9-inch frozen pie crust
- ¼ lb. sliced ham, chopped
- 1½ cups shredded Swiss cheese

1 Line a rimmed baking sheet with foil, place it in oven and preheat to 375°F. Mist a medium skillet with cooking spray and warm it over medium heat. Cook spinach, stirring often, until wilted. Remove spinach to a paper towel–lined plate and pat dry.

2 In a large bowl, combine eggs, half-and-half and salt and whisk until well mixed. Arrange spinach on bottom of pie crust. Scatter ham over spinach. Sprinkle cheese over ham. Pour egg mixture into shell.

3 Place quiche on baking sheet and bake until filling is set and crust is golden, about 40 minutes. Let stand approximately 10 minutes before slicing into wedges and serving hot.

PER SERVING: 298 Cal., 21g Fat (10g Sat.), 202mg Chol., 0g Fiber, 15g Pro., 12g Carb., 562mg Sod.

SMART TIPS

✳ **Get the best texture.** Cooking the quiche on a preheated baking sheet helps crisp the bottom of the crust.

✳ **Save leftovers.** Refrigerate leftover quiche covered tightly with plastic wrap. Warm a slice in the microwave for breakfast the next day.

CHICKEN & TURKEY

BEEF & LAMB

PORK

FISH

VEGETABLES

Pork and Peanut Stir-Fry

Prep: 10 min.
Cook: 10 min.
Serves: 4
Cost per serving:

$1.78

- ¼ cup low-sodium chicken broth or water
- 1 Tbsp. soy sauce
- 1 Tbsp. rice vinegar
- 2 tsp. cornstarch
- 2 tsp. vegetable oil
- 1 2-inch piece fresh ginger, peeled and grated
- 5 scallions, chopped, white parts separated from green
- 2 8-oz. boneless pork chops, cut into thin strips
- ¼ cup plus 1 Tbsp. dry-roasted peanuts, chopped

1 In a small bowl, mix broth, soy sauce, vinegar and cornstarch together. Set aside.

2 Warm oil in a wok or large skillet over medium-high heat. Add ginger and white part of scallions. Cook, stirring constantly, until scallions are just softened, about 1 minute.

3 Add pork and cook, tossing with tongs, until firm and no longer pink, 5 minutes.

4 Stir in sauce and ¼ cup peanuts.

Cook, stirring constantly, until sauce is thickened and pork is heated through, 2 minutes. If sauce is too thick, add broth, 1 Tbsp. at a time, until it reaches desired consistency. Top with green part of scallions and remaining peanuts.

PER SERVING: 271 Cal., 15g Fat (3g Sat.), 63mg Chol., 1g Fiber, 29g Pro., 5g Carb., 215mg Sod.

MARK THOMAS, FOOD STYLING: LYNN MILLER

Ham and Gruyère Stratas

Prep: 10 min.
Chill: 6 hr.
Bake: 40 min.
Serves: 6
Cost per serving:

$2.31

- 8 large eggs
- 1 Tbsp. Dijon mustard
- 2 tsp. salt
- 2 cups whole milk
- 2 cups half-and-half
- 10 slices white sandwich bread, crusts trimmed, cut into 1-inch pieces
- ½ lb. sliced ham, chopped
- 1 bunch scallions, white and light green parts, chopped
- 2 cups shredded Gruyère (about 5 oz.)

1 Grease 6 1-cup ramekins. In a large bowl, whisk together eggs, mustard and salt. Whisk in milk and half-and-half. Mix in bread, ham, scallions and 1 cup cheese. Pour mixture into prepared dishes. Cover with plastic wrap and refrigerate for at least 6 hours and up to 10 hours.

2 Preheat oven to 375°F and remove stratas from refrigerator while oven heats. Bake stratas uncovered for 30 minutes, then sprinkle remaining cheese over tops, and bake 10 minutes longer. Let stand 5 minutes before serving.

PER SERVING: 599 Cal., 30g Fat (15g Sat.), 369mg Chol., 4g Fiber, 34g Pro., 47g Carb., 1,779mg Sod.

Tandoori Roasted Pork Tenderloin

FRANCES JANISCH; FOOD STYLING: LYNN MILLER

SMART TIP

✱ Give it a rest.
Don't slice the pork right away. The meat will continue to cook when it comes out of the oven. As it rests, the meat's internal temperature rises until it reaches a perfect 155°F, and the juices will distribute, making for a tastier roast.

Prep: 5 min.
Cook: 25 min.
Serves: 4
Cost per serving:

$1.76

- 1 Tbsp. fresh lemon juice
- ½ cup plain yogurt
- 2 Tbsp. chopped fresh ginger
- 2 cloves garlic, chopped
- Salt
- ¼ tsp. ground cumin
- ¼ tsp. ground coriander
- ¼ tsp. cayenne pepper
- ¼ tsp. turmeric
- 1 1-lb. pork tenderloin, rinsed and patted dry

1 Set oven racks in top and middle positions and preheat oven to 450°F. Mix lemon juice, yogurt, ginger, garlic, ½ tsp. salt, cumin, coriander, cayenne and turmeric in a blender until smooth.

2 Place pork in a stainless steel or glass bowl and spoon half of yogurt mixture on top, turning pork to coat. Let stand while oven heats.

3 Transfer tenderloin to a rimmed baking sheet, letting excess marinade drip back into bowl. Roast on middle rack for 10 minutes, turn over, pour remaining yogurt mixture over pork and continue to roast until an instant-read thermometer placed in center of pork reads 145°F, 8 to 10 minutes longer.

4 Set oven to broil, place pork on baking sheet on top rack and broil for 2 to 3 minutes, turning once, until both sides are lightly browned. Transfer to cutting board, tent with foil and let rest 5 minutes before slicing and serving.

PER SERVING: 167 Cal., 5g Fat (2g Sat.), 78mg Chol., 0g Fiber, 25g Pro., 4g Carb., 367mg Sod.

Cheesy Baked Penne with Ham and Broccoli

Prep: 20 min.
Bake: 30 min.
Serves: 6
Cost per serving:

$1.94

- Salt and pepper
- 8 oz. penne
- 2 cups chopped broccoli florets
- 5 Tbsp. unsalted butter
- ½ cup panko (or other coarse bread crumbs)
- ¼ cup all-purpose flour
- 3 cups low-fat milk, at room temperature
- ½ tsp. paprika
- ⅛ tsp. nutmeg
- 1 cup shredded Gruyère or Swiss cheese
- 2 cups shredded sharp Cheddar
- ¼ cup grated Parmesan
- 4 oz. ham, cut into 1-inch strips

1 Preheat oven to 375°F; grease a 9-by-13-inch baking dish.

Bring a pot of salted water to a boil. Cook pasta for 7 minutes. Add broccoli; cook 3 to 4 minutes longer. Drain, rinse with cold water; drain again. Pour into casserole dish.

2 In a pan over medium heat, melt butter. Remove 1 Tbsp. melted butter; stir into panko in a bowl. Set aside. Add flour to pan; whisk until bubbling, about 1 minute. Whisk in milk. Add paprika, pepper, nutmeg and salt. Stir until sauce thickens, 6 to 8 minutes. Remove from heat. Stir Gruyère and 1½ cups Cheddar into sauce until smooth. Stir in ham.

3 Stir sauce into pasta and broccoli. Sprinkle with remaining Cheddar and reserved panko. Bake until crumbs are browned and sauce is bubbling, 30 minutes. Let stand for 5 minutes; serve.

PER SERVING: 623 Cal., 36g Fat (20g Sat.), 107mg Chol., 3g Fiber, 30g Pro., 45g Carb., 860mg Sod.

Hearty Minestrone with Shells

Prep: 20 min.
Cook: 40 min.
Serves: 8
Cost per serving:

$1.53

- 8 oz. Italian sausage, casings removed
- 1 Tbsp. olive oil
- 1 onion, chopped
- 3 cloves garlic, chopped
- 3 stalks celery, chopped
- 1 carrot, chopped
- 4 cups low-sodium chicken broth
- 1 15-oz. can diced tomatoes with juices
- 4 oz. green beans, trimmed, cut into 1-inch pieces
- 2 cups chopped fresh Swiss chard
- 1 15-oz. can cannellini beans, rinsed and drained
- 6 oz. medium-size pasta shells
- ½ cup grated Parmesan
- Salt and pepper

1 In a large pot over medium heat, cook sausage, stirring and breaking up with a wooden spoon until no traces of pink remain, 6 to 8 minutes. Transfer meat to paper towels; drain fat from pot. Add olive oil, onion, garlic, celery and carrot and cook, stirring, until vegetables have softened, 6 to 8 minutes.

2 Stir in broth, tomatoes and 3 cups water and bring to a simmer. Add green beans and chard and simmer until very soft, about 20 minutes. Stir in beans, reserved sausage and pasta and simmer, stirring occasionally, until pasta is al dente, 8 to 10 minutes.

3 Stir in Parmesan and season with salt and pepper. Ladle into bowls and serve.

PER SERVING: 300 Cal., 13g Fat (5g Sat.), 27mg Chol., 4g Fiber, 15g Pro., 31g Carb., 1,056mg Sod.

RYAN BENYI, FOOD STYLING: LYNN MILLER (2)

CHICKEN & TURKEY

BEEF & LAMB

PORK

FISH

VEGETABLES

Enjoy a taste of the tropics
with coconut shrimp served over
fragrant basmati rice (page 128).

CHICKEN &
TURKEY

BEEF &
LAMB

PORK

FISH

VEGETABLES

Fish

We all know we're supposed to be eating fish—it's full of nutrients, particularly lean protein and the important omega-3 fatty acids we hear so much about. But fish can be intimidating. There are so many varieties and different ways to cook them, and it can be pricey. Luckily, using frozen and canned fish and a dash of creativity, it's not hard to make budget-friendly recipes that the whole family can enjoy.

127 Fish Stick Tacos

127 Maple-Glazed Salmon Fillets

128 Coconut Shrimp and Rice

129 Tuna Noodle Casserole

130 Tortellini Salad with Salmon and Peas

131 Italian Tuna Melts

133 Niçoise Pasta Salad

Fish Stick Tacos

Prep: 5 min.
Cook: 16 min.
Serves: 4
Cost per serving:

$1.76

- 8 6-inch corn tortillas
- 1 11-oz. box frozen breaded fish sticks
- ½ tsp. chili powder
- 5 cups coleslaw mix (cabbage and carrots)
- ¼ cup reduced-fat mayonnaise
- ¼ tsp. chipotle chili (canned in adobo sauce), seeded and chopped
- 2 Tbsp. lime juice
- Salt
- 1 cup tomato salsa

1 Preheat oven to 475°F. Line a baking sheet with foil. Stack tortillas in a microwave-safe dish. Lightly dampen a clean kitchen towel; wring out any excess water. Cover tortillas with towel and microwave at 50 percent for 2 to 3 minutes, until warmed. Keep covered until ready to use.

2 Arrange fish sticks on baking sheet and sprinkle with chili powder. Bake until fish sticks are crispy, 11 to 13 minutes.

3 While fish sticks are baking, stir together coleslaw mix, mayonnaise, chipotle and lime juice in a medium bowl. Season with salt.

4 Place a tortilla on a work surface and top with a bit of slaw mixture. Add 2 fish sticks and top with a spoonful of salsa. Fold up taco. Repeat with remaining tortillas, slaw mixture, fish sticks and salsa. Serve immediately.

PER SERVING: 390 Cal., 17g Fat (3g Sat.), 30mg Chol., 8g Fiber, 13g Pro., 49g Carb., 1,301mg Sod.

SMART TIPS

* **Portion the fish.** If your favorite brand of fish sticks doesn't come pre-portioned in eight pieces, simply cut up the fish to divide it among the tacos.

* **Wrap it up.** Feel free to use flour tortillas instead of corn, if you prefer. If your market has only a larger size, make the tacos into burritos and serve 1 to each person instead of 2 tacos.

Maple-Glazed Salmon Fillets

Prep: 5 min.
Cook: 20 min.
Serves: 4
Cost per serving:

$2.41

- 2 Tbsp. pure maple syrup
- 2 Tbsp. Dijon mustard
- ¼ tsp. garlic powder
- 4 6-oz. salmon fillets
- Salt

1 Preheat oven to 400°F. Line a large rimmed baking sheet with parchment paper or nonstick foil. In a small bowl, stir together maple syrup, mustard and garlic powder until well combined.

2 Place salmon, skin side down, on lined baking sheet; sprinkle lightly with salt and brush with maple syrup mixture. Bake until fish is just cooked through and flakes easily with a fork, about 20 minutes. Remove skin, if desired. Serve immediately.

PER SERVING: 276 Cal., 11g Fat (2g Sat.), 94mg Chol., 0g Fiber, 34g Pro., 8g Carb., 546mg Sod.

Coconut Shrimp and Rice

Prep: 5 min.
Cook: 22 min.
Serves: 6
Cost per serving:

$1.48

- **1½ cups basmati rice**
- **1 Tbsp. unsalted butter**
- **1 clove garlic, finely chopped**
- **¼ tsp. crushed red pepper**
- **12 oz. medium shrimp, peeled and deveined**
- **1 cup low-sodium chicken broth**
- **1 cup canned coconut milk (shake before opening)**
- **¼ cup fresh lime juice (from about 3 limes)**
- **½ tsp. salt**
- **¼ cup finely chopped fresh cilantro**

1 Rinse and drain rice several times in cold water to remove excess starch. Melt butter in a large saucepan over medium-high heat. Add garlic, crushed red pepper and shrimp and sauté until shrimp is cooked through, 3 to 4 minutes total. Transfer shrimp mixture to a plate and cover with foil to keep warm.

2 Add rice to saucepan and cook, stirring, until fragrant and lightly toasted, about 3 minutes. Stir in broth, coconut milk, lime juice and salt, and bring to a boil over high heat. Reduce heat to low, cover pan and cook until rice is tender, about 15 minutes. Stir in cilantro, and serve topped with shrimp.

PER SERVING: 318 Cal., 11g Fat (8g Sat.), 90mg Chol., 1g Fiber, 16g Pro., 41g Carb., 377mg Sod.

ALAN RICHARDSON, FOOD STYLING: STEPHANA BOTTOM

Tuna Noodle Casserole

Prep: 15 min.
Bake: 30 min.
Serves: 4
Cost per serving:

$1.46

- 3 Tbsp. unsalted butter
- 3 Tbsp. all-purpose flour
- 1 cup low-fat milk
- 1 cup low-sodium chicken broth
- Salt and pepper
- 8 oz. egg noodles
- 2 3-oz. cans tuna packed in oil, drained
- 5 oz. frozen green peas
- ⅓ cup bread crumbs
- ½ cup shredded Cheddar
- 2 Tbsp. vegetable oil

1 Preheat oven to 375°F; grease an 11-by-7-inch 2-quart baking dish.

2 Melt butter in a small saucepan over medium-high heat. Add flour and whisk until smooth and blended, about 2 minutes. Whisk in milk and broth. Cook, whisking often, until mixture turns into a thick, smooth sauce, about 10 minutes. Season with salt and pepper.

3 Bring a large pot of salted water to a boil. Add noodles and cook until almost done, about 5 minutes. Drain noodles thoroughly in a colander and return to pot. Stir in sauce, tuna and peas. Transfer to baking dish and spread mixture evenly.

4 Combine bread crumbs and cheese in a small bowl; sprinkle over mixture in baking dish. Drizzle evenly with vegetable oil and bake until casserole is golden brown and bubbly, 20 to 25 minutes. Let stand for 5 minutes before serving. Serve hot.

PER SERVING: 633 Cal., 29g Fat (11g Sat.), 113mg Chol., 4g Fiber, 29g Pro., 63g Carb., 891mg Sod.

SMART TIP

❋ **Dress it up.** Stir in ¼ cup chopped roasted red peppers or some chopped cooked broccoli for more color and flavor.

RYAN BENYI; FOOD STYLING: ANDREA STEINBERG

CHICKEN &
TURKEY

BEEF &
LAMB

PORK

FISH

VEGETABLES

* **Get a head start.** After you make the salad, cover it with foil or plastic wrap and chill for up to 6 hours.

* **Lower the calories.** Make a lighter version by replacing the tortellini with regular pasta. A short shape such as fusilli, farfalle or penne works best.

* **Add a splash of color.** Toss in a few handfuls of halved cherry tomatoes with the salmon and basil.

* **Switch the herbs.** Along with the basil, try including a variety of fresh herbs such as parsley, thyme and tarragon.

Tortellini Salad with Salmon and Peas

Prep: 5 min.
Cook: 22 min.
Serves: 6
Cost per serving:

$1.88

- **8 oz. fresh salmon fillet, skin removed**
- **Salt and pepper**

- **1 lb. fresh cheese tortellini**
- **¾ cup light mayonnaise**
- **2 Tbsp. fresh lemon juice**
- **1 cup frozen peas, defrosted**
- **½ cup finely chopped fresh basil leaves**

1 Preheat grill to high; oil grate. Sprinkle salmon with pepper. Grill salmon, turning once, until cooked through and easily flaked with a fork, 12 to 15 minutes total.

2 Bring a large pot of salted water to a boil. Cook tortellini according to package label directions, about 7 minutes. Drain and run under cold water, then drain again.

3 In a large bowl, whisk together mayonnaise and lemon juice. Mix in tortellini and peas; toss to coat. Season with salt. Gently stir in salmon and basil and serve.

PER SERVING: 406 Cal., 18g Fat (4g Sat.), 60mg Chol., 3g Fiber, 20g Pro., 42g Carb., 781mg Sod.

SMART TIPS

* Swap cheeses.
Creamy mozzarella works well on these hearty sandwiches, but a stronger cheese, such as provolone, is also delicious.

* Boost the flavor.
Stir in a few chopped roasted red peppers for extra flavor and color.

* Pick a side. A mild vegetable, such as peas, goes best with these sandwiches.

Italian Tuna Melts

Prep: 10 min.
Bake: 2 min.
Serves: 6
Cost per serving:

$1.61

- 1 loaf Italian or French bread (about 14 oz.)
- 3 6-oz. cans solid white tuna in water, drained
- 3 Tbsp. extra-virgin olive oil
- 1½ Tbsp. fresh lemon juice
- 1 Tbsp. finely chopped fresh parsley
- ¼ cup kalamata or other black olives, pitted and chopped
- Salt and pepper
- 4 oz. shredded mozzarella

1 Set oven rack 4 inches from broiler and preheat. Line a rimmed baking sheet with foil. Slice bread loaf into thirds, then slice each third in half lengthwise so you have 6 equal pieces.

2 Flake tuna into a medium bowl. Stir in oil, lemon juice, parsley and olives. Season with salt and pepper. Spread tuna mixture evenly over each piece of bread and sprinkle with cheese.

3 Place sandwiches on baking sheet and broil until cheese is bubbling, 1 to 2 minutes. Serve immediately.

PER SERVING: 411 Cal., 14g Fat (3g Sat.), 7mg Chol., 2g Fiber, 34g Pro., 36g Carb., 1,211mg Sod.

RYAN BENYI FOOD STYLING: STEPHANA BOTTOM

Niçoise Pasta Salad

Prep: 10 min.
Cook: 10 min.
Serves: 6
Cost per serving:

$1.61

- Salt
- 1 lb. penne or other short pasta
- ½ lb. green beans, trimmed
- 6 Tbsp. olive oil
- 1 Tbsp. red wine vinegar
- 2 6-oz. cans tuna packed in water, drained
- 2 cups cherry tomatoes, halved
- ½ cup black olives, pitted and chopped
- ¼ cup finely chopped fresh parsley
- 1 Tbsp. capers, drained

1 Bring a large pot of salted water to boil over high heat. Add pasta and cook until almost tender, about 8 minutes. Add green beans to pot and continue to boil until beans and pasta are both tender, about 2 minutes longer. Drain, reserving ¼ cup cooking water. Run pasta and beans under cold water and drain again. Set pasta and green beans aside.

2 In a large bowl, whisk together oil, vinegar and ¼ tsp. salt. Stir in tuna, tomatoes, olives, parsley and capers.

3 Add pasta and green beans to bowl. Stir, adding reserved cooking water to moisten as necessary, and serve.
PER SERVING: 501 Cal., 18g Fat (2g Sat.), 25mg Chol., 4g Fiber, 23g Pro., 60g Carb., 379mg Sod.

SMART TIPS

✳ **Stick to tradition.** To make this even more like a classic Niçoise salad, hard-boil 6 eggs, quarter them and add to each portion before serving.

✳ **Swap meat.** If you have leftover grilled chicken in the fridge, chop it up and substitute it for the tuna. Or make the salad vegetarian by adding a can of white beans or chickpeas (rinse and drain first).

✳ **Make it even more healthful.** Boost the fiber and nutrients by using whole-wheat pasta. If your family balks, use half whole-wheat and half regular to get them used to the taste.

MAKE PERFECT PASTA

Few things please the family more and make for quicker weeknight meals than pasta. Cook it up the right way.

1 **Choose the proper pot.** Start with a pot big enough to hold all the pasta and plenty of water. Using a too-small pot can cause the noodles to stick to the bottom or sides and cook less evenly. Bring the water  to a full rolling boil before adding the pasta. Add a generous pinch of salt once the water is boiling to season the pasta.

2 **Keep an eye on it.** Add the noodles to the pot all at once and stir well to completely cover with water. Different pasta shapes require different cooking times, so set a timer based on the package directions for the type  you're cooking. Watch it carefully—even a minute of extra cooking can leave your noodles mushy. Use a fork to grab a piece of pasta out of the pot and take a bite to test for doneness.

3 **Drain, toss and serve.** When the pasta is cooked, drain it well, toss or top it with your favorite sauce and serve it immediately. Letting pasta sit too long can make it turn mushy. If you're making a cold  pasta salad, rinse the drained noodles with ice-cold water to stop them from cooking, then dress, cover and refrigerate the salad.

CHICKEN & TURKEY

BEEF & LAMB

PORK

FISH

VEGETABLES

Serve stuffed shells with ricotta and spinach (page 167)—no one will miss the meat.

Vegetables

Once relegated to the sidelines, vegetables are taking their rightful place at the center of many dinner plates. Even the most dedicated meat-and-potatoes fans are finding that vegetable-based dinners—from hearty stews and soups to comforting pastas—can be satisfying. And along with being nutritious, veggie dishes are easy on the wallet.

136 Corn and Cheese Enchiladas
137 Sautéed Chickpeas with Broccoli and Parmesan
138 Pita Bread and Pea Salad
139 Baked Pasta Primavera
141 Crispy Ravioli
141 Fried Brown Rice with Broccoli and Tofu
142 Broccoli and Double Cheese Calzones
143 Pasta with Chickpeas and Broccoli
144 Pasta with Ricotta and Edamame
145 Broccoli-and-Cheddar Mini Quiches
147 Refried Bean Tostadas
148 Weeknight Ravioli Lasagna
149 Broccoli-Orzo Salad
150 Pasta with Cauliflower and Olives
151 Chili-Cheese Biscuit Pies
153 Pasta with Tomatoes and Mozzarella
154 Slow-Cooker Eggplant and Tomato Sauce with Pasta

155 Corn, Black Bean and Pepper-Jack Burritos
156 Spinach-Ricotta Skillet Lasagna
157 Black Bean Burgers
159 Pasta with Yogurt Pesto
159 Spinach-and-Cheese Quiche
160 Quick Mushroom-Barley Soup
161 Cavatelli with Spicy Broccoli
163 Cheddar-and-Tomato Bread Pudding
163 Baked Eggs in Bread Bowls
164 Tacos with Sweet Potatoes and Pinto Beans
165 Broccoli-Cheese Soup
166 Pasta-and-Bean Soup
167 Spinach-and-Ricotta Stuffed Shells
169 Broccoli-and-Feta Frittata
170 Slow-Cooker Peanut–Sweet Potato Stew
171 Vegetable Moussaka

Corn and Cheese Enchiladas

Prep: 21 min.
Bake: 20 min.
Serves: 4
Cost per serving:

$1.98

- 8 6-inch corn tortillas
- 1 Tbsp. vegetable oil
- 5 scallions, white and light green parts, chopped
- 2 cloves garlic, finely chopped
- 1½ cups fresh corn kernels (from 2 medium ears)
- ½ cup whole milk
- Salt
- 2 cups grated pepper Jack
- 1 10-oz. can enchilada sauce

1 Preheat oven to 350°F. Stack tortillas, wrap in foil and bake until softened, 8 to 10 minutes.

2 While tortillas are baking, grease a 7-by-11-inch glass baking dish. Warm 1 Tbsp. oil in a large skillet over medium-high heat. Add scallions and garlic and cook, stirring, until fragrant, about 1 minute. Stir in corn and milk and cook, stirring occasionally, until thickened, 7 to 10 minutes. Season with salt.

3 Remove tortillas from foil. Set aside

½ cup cheese. Spoon a heaping tablespoon of corn mixture in center of a tortilla. Sprinkle with a heaping tablespoon of cheese. Roll up tortilla and set in dish, seam side down. Repeat with remaining tortillas, corn mixture and cheese, overlapping them

slightly. Pour enchilada sauce over tortillas and sprinkle with reserved ½ cup cheese. Bake until bubbling, about 20 minutes. Let stand for 5 minutes before serving.
PER SERVING: 457 Cal., 25g Fat (13g Sat.), 64mg Chol.,5g Fiber, 20g Pro., 41g Carb., 1,323mg Sod.

SMART TIP

✳ **Don't forget the sides.** Serve these tasty enchiladas with chopped fresh cilantro, sliced avocado, scallions and salsa.

SMART TIPS

✳ **Increase the protein.** Add cooked shrimp or chicken, or cubed tofu, to make this dish more substantial.

✳ **Take a shortcut.** You can use frozen broccoli florets in this dish if you prefer. There's no need to thaw them, but the dish might take an extra minute or two to cook.

Sautéed Chickpeas with Broccoli and Parmesan

Prep: 5 min.
Cook: 11 min.
Serves: 4
Cost per serving:

80¢

- 2 Tbsp. olive oil
- 1 small onion, thinly sliced
- 4 cloves garlic, thinly sliced
- Salt and pepper
- 1½ small heads broccoli, including stalks, trimmed and chopped (about 2 cups)
- 1 10.5-oz. can chickpeas, drained and rinsed
- ⅓ cup chicken or vegetable broth
- ¼ tsp. crushed red pepper
- ⅓ cup Parmesan shavings

1 In a large skillet (preferably one with a lid), warm olive oil over medium heat until hot. Add onion and garlic, season with salt, and cook, stirring often, until onion becomes transparent and garlic just begins to turn golden brown, 4 to 5 minutes.

2 Toss in broccoli; sauté for 3 minutes. Add chickpeas, broth and red pepper. Stir once, cover and cook for 3 minutes more, just to heat through and finish cooking broccoli.

3 Uncover skillet, season with pepper, sprinkle with Parmesan and serve. Pass extra Parmesan on the side, if desired.

PER SERVING: 186 Cal., 10g Fat (2g Sat.), 5mg Chol., 5g Fiber, 9g Pro., 16g Carb., 855mg Sod.

Pita Bread and Pea Salad

Prep: 25 min.
Bake: 20 min.
Serves: 6
Cost per serving:

$1.64

- 3 pitas
- ⅓ cup plus 1 Tbsp. extra-virgin olive oil
- Salt and pepper
- ¼ cup lemon juice
- 2 stalks celery, thinly sliced
- 1 cup frozen peas, defrosted, drained and patted dry
- ½ red onion, thinly sliced
- 1 cup cucumber, peeled, seeded and diced
- 1 cup baby spinach
- 5 oz. crumbled feta
- 1 Tbsp. chopped fresh mint
- 1 Tbsp. chopped fresh parsley

1 Preheat oven to 350°F. Brush both sides of pitas with 1 Tbsp. olive oil; sprinkle with salt and pepper. Cut pitas into strips, 1 inch wide and 3 inches long. Bake on a baking sheet until golden brown, about 20 minutes.

2 Whisk lemon juice and ⅓ cup oil in a small bowl and season with salt. Place toasted pita in a large salad bowl. Add celery, peas, onion and cucumber. Toss with lemon vinaigrette.

3 Fold in spinach, feta, mint and parsley. Season with pepper and serve.

PER SERVING: 227 Cal., 19g Fat (6g Sat.), 21mg Chol., 2g Fiber, 5g Pro., 9g Carb., 477mg Sod.

Baked Pasta Primavera

SMART TIPS

❋ **Add meat.** Stir in crumbled cooked sausage to make this dish even heartier. Or use vegetable broth instead of chicken broth to make it vegetarian.

❋ **Make it crunchy.** Use panko instead of ordinary bread crumbs to give the topping a boost.

❋ **Pick a shape.** This recipe calls for ziti, but any short pasta shape will work.

Prep: 20 min.

Cook: 25 min.

Serves: 4

Cost per serving:

$1.61

- 4 Tbsp. unsalted butter
- 3 Tbsp. all-purpose flour
- 1 cup milk
- 1 cup low-sodium chicken broth
- Salt and pepper
- ¾ cup grated Parmesan
- 8 oz. ziti
- 1 1-lb. package mixed frozen vegetables
- ⅓ cup plain bread crumbs

1 Preheat oven to 375°F; lightly grease a 2-quart (11-by-7-inch) baking dish.

2 Melt 3 Tbsp. butter in a small saucepan over medium-high heat. Add flour and stir until blended, about 2 minutes. Whisk in milk and broth. Cook, stirring often, until mixture forms a thick, smooth sauce, about 10 minutes. Season with salt and pepper. Stir in ¼ cup Parmesan.

3 Bring a large pot of salted water to a boil. Add ziti and cook until softened, about 5 minutes. Add vegetables and bring back to a boil. Cook until pasta is almost done, about 3 minutes longer. Drain and return to pot.

4 Pour sauce over pasta and vegetables and mix well. Transfer to baking dish, spreading evenly. Combine remaining Parmesan and bread crumbs in a small dish. Melt remaining 1 Tbsp. butter, stir into bread-crumb mixture and sprinkle over top of casserole. Bake until casserole is bubbly and top is golden brown, 20 to 25 minutes.

PER SERVING: 519 Cal., 19g Fat (11g Sat.), 50mg Chol., 5g Fiber, 19g Pro., 67g Carb., 1,083mg Sod.

Crispy Ravioli

Prep: 5 min.
Cook: 15 min.
Serves: 4
Cost per serving:

$1.69

- Vegetable oil, for frying
- 1 large egg
- 2 Tbsp. milk
- ⅔ cup seasoned bread crumbs
- 24 refrigerated cheese ravioli
- ¼ cup grated Parmesan
- 2 cups jarred marinara sauce

1 Pour enough vegetable oil into a large, deep pot so that it reaches a depth of 1 inch. Warm oil over medium heat until a deep-fry thermometer registers 325°F. Line a baking sheet with parchment or foil, and line a plate with paper towels.

2 While vegetable oil is heating, whisk together egg and milk in a shallow bowl. Place bread crumbs in a separate shallow bowl. Working in batches, dip ravioli into egg mixture, allowing excess to drip back into bowl, then coat with bread crumbs. Place coated ravioli on baking sheet. Discard remaining bread crumbs.

3 Fry ravioli in batches, turning occasionally, until golden brown, about 3 minutes total. Be careful not to crowd ravioli in pan, and make sure oil comes back to 325°F before adding another batch of ravioli. Transfer fried ravioli to lined plate to drain. Sprinkle fried ravioli with grated Parmesan.

4 Warm marinara sauce in a microwave or in a pan over medium-low heat. Spoon sauce into 4 small bowls. Serve crispy ravioli with warmed marinara on the side.

PER SERVING: 482 Cal., 19g Fat (6g Sat.), 99mg Chol., 3g Fiber, 17g Pro., 61g Carb., 1,105mg Sod.

Fried Brown Rice with Broccoli and Tofu

Prep: 10 min.
Cook: 1 hr. 20 min
Serves: 4
Cost per serving:

$1.33

- 1 cup long-grain brown rice
- Salt and pepper
- 2 Tbsp. vegetable oil
- 1 clove garlic, minced
- 2 Tbsp. grated fresh ginger
- 2 cups small broccoli florets
- 2 Tbsp. soy sauce
- 8 oz. firm tofu, cut into small cubes

1 Stir rice, 2¼ cups water and a pinch of salt together in a medium saucepan and bring to a boil over high heat. Reduce heat to medium-low, cover and cook until rice is tender and liquid has been absorbed, 45 to 50 minutes. Remove from heat, fluff with a fork and let stand, covered, for 10 minutes.

2 Warm oil in a large skillet over medium-high heat. Add garlic and ginger and sauté until fragrant, about 30 seconds. Add broccoli and cook, stirring, for 2 minutes. Pour in ½ cup water and soy sauce. Cook, stirring often, until

broccoli is softened yet slightly crisp, about 12 minutes. Add rice and tofu to skillet and cook, stirring, until heated through, about 3 minutes. Season with salt and pepper. Serve warm.

PER SERVING: 307 Cal., 11g Fat (1g Sat.), 0mg Chol., 3g Fiber, 10g Pro., 41g Carb., 767mg Sod.

SMART TIPS

✳ **Switch cheeses.** For a different flavor, try smoked mozzarella or pepper Jack.

✳ **Swap the veggies.** Try these calzones with chopped spinach or carrots, or add some sliced ham.

✳ **Get fresh.** Instead of frozen, buy freshly made dough from a pizzeria.

Broccoli and Double Cheese Calzones

Prep: 10 min.
Bake: 15 min.
Serves: 4
Cost per serving:

$1.49

- 1½ cups broccoli florets
- 1 large clove garlic, minced
- ⅔ cup ricotta
- 4 oz. mozzarella, coarsely grated (1 cup)
- 1 large egg yolk
- Salt and pepper
- 1 lb. frozen pizza dough, thawed
- 1½ Tbsp. olive oil

1 Preheat oven to 450°F. Bring 1 inch of water to a boil in a small pot. Place broccoli in a steamer basket, place steamer basket in pot, cover and steam until tender, 4 to 5 minutes. Let cool slightly, coarsely chop, and place in a medium bowl. Stir in garlic, ricotta, mozzarella and egg yolk; season generously with salt and pepper.

2 Divide pizza dough into 4 portions and use a rolling pin to roll each into an 8-inch circle. Place a quarter of broccoli mixture in center of a round, fold dough in half, and then seal by rolling edges together toward center and crimping. Using a sharp knife, cut 2 small slits in top of calzone to let steam escape. Repeat with remaining dough and broccoli mixture.

Brush calzones with olive oil.

3 Mist a large, rimmed baking sheet with nonstick cooking spray. Place calzones on baking sheet, spacing so they don't touch, and bake in center of oven until golden and risen, 13 to 15 minutes. Serve immediately, with warm tomato sauce on the side for dipping, if desired.
PER SERVING: 559 Cal., 35g Fat (14g Sat.), 112mg Chol., 4g Fiber, 25g Pro., 37g Carb., 1,063mg Sod.

Pasta with Chickpeas and Broccoli

Prep: 5 min.
Cook: 20 min.
Serves: 6
Cost per serving:

79¢

- ¼ cup olive oil
- 3 cloves garlic, finely chopped
- ½ cup plain bread crumbs
- ¼ tsp. crushed red pepper
- Salt
- 1 lb. penne or other small, short pasta
- 4 cups small broccoli florets (from 1 large head broccoli)
- ¼ cup low-sodium chicken broth
- 1 15.5-oz. can chickpeas, drained and rinsed

1 Bring a large pot of water to boil over high heat. Warm oil over medium heat in a large skillet. Add garlic and cook, stirring, until fragrant, about 30 seconds. Stir in bread crumbs, crushed red pepper and ½ tsp. salt and cook, stirring, until bread crumbs are toasted, 2 to 3 minutes. Remove from heat.

2 Add 1 Tbsp. salt and pasta to pot with boiling water and cook until almost tender, about 10 minutes. Add broccoli to pot and continue to boil until broccoli and pasta are both tender, about 2 minutes longer. Drain and return pasta and broccoli to pot.

3 Add chicken broth and chickpeas to pot with pasta and broccoli, return pot to heat and stir until broth is heated through, about 2 minutes. Add bread-crumb mixture to pot with pasta mixture and toss to coat. Serve immediately.

PER SERVING: 459 Cal., 12g Fat (1g Sat.), 0mg Chol., 7g Fiber, 15g Pro., 74g Carb., 456mg Sod.

SMART TIP

✳ **Choose your broccoli.** If you prefer to use frozen florets, simply defrost, drain and toss in with pasta and broth.

Pasta with Ricotta and Edamame

Prep: 10 min.
Cook: 12 min.
Serves: 6
Cost per serving:

$1.27

- **1 15-oz. container ricotta**
- **½ cup grated Parmesan**
- **Salt and pepper**
- **1 lb. fusilli or other short pasta**
- **2 cups frozen shelled edamame**
- **⅓ cup finely chopped fresh mint**

1 Stir together ricotta, Parmesan and salt in a large bowl.

2 Bring a large pot of salted water to boil. Cook pasta until just al dente, 11 to 12 minutes (or as package label directs). Add edamame to pot for final 1 minute of pasta cooking time. Reserve 1 cup cooking water and drain pasta and edamame. Add pasta to bowl with cheese mixture along with ½ cup cooking water and stir. If mixture is too dry, add more water, 1 Tbsp. at a time, until creamy. Stir in mint, season with salt and pepper and serve immediately.

PER SERVING: 351 Cal., 15g Fat (2g Sat.), 38mg Chol., 5g Fiber, 25g Pro., 31g Carb., 588mg Sod.

Broccoli-and-Cheddar Mini Quiches

SMART TIPS

✳ **Swap fillings.** Try a different cheese or swap another vegetable for the broccoli, depending on what your family likes. Or make classic quiche lorraine with crumbled bacon and shredded Swiss cheese.

✳ **Save time.** Use your microwave: Place the broccoli and a bit of water in a microwave-safe bowl, cover and cook on high until just tender, about 3 minutes.

Prep: 10 min.
Bake: 25 min.
Serves: 4
Cost per serving:

$1.57

- 2 cups broccoli florets
- 1 cup milk (do not use skim)
- 1 cup heavy cream
- 2 large eggs plus 2 large egg yolks
- 1 cup grated Cheddar
- ½ tsp. salt
- ½ tsp. pepper
- ¼ tsp. ground nutmeg

1 Preheat oven to 350°F and line a large rimmed baking sheet with foil. Grease 8 cups in a 12-cup muffin tin and set aside. Pour 1 inch of water into a large saucepan and put in a steamer basket. Place broccoli in steamer basket, cover pot, turn heat to high and let cook until broccoli is just tender, 5 to 6 minutes. Let broccoli cool slightly, then chop into small pieces.

2 In a medium bowl, whisk together milk, cream, eggs and egg yolks. Stir in cheese, salt, pepper and nutmeg. Add chopped broccoli.

3 Put muffin tin on baking sheet, then ladle egg mixture into prepared muffin cups, filling each cup. Bake until lightly browned and no longer jiggly in center, about 25 minutes. Let cool slightly, then run a knife around each quiche. Put a clean baking sheet on top of muffin pan and invert to unmold quiches. Serve warm or at room temperature. **PER SERVING:** 435 Cal., 39g Fat (23g Sat.), 332mg Chol., 0g Fiber, 16g Pro., 7g Carb., 535mg Sod.

Refried Bean Tostadas

Prep: 10 min.
Cook: 10 min.
Yield: 6
Cost per serving:

75¢

- 6 6-inch flour or corn tortillas
- ¾ cup fat-free refried beans
- ¾ cup jarred red salsa
- 1 cup shredded Cheddar (about 2½ oz.)
- 1 Tbsp. finely chopped fresh cilantro
- 1 cup shredded Romaine lettuce
- 2 Tbsp. sour cream

1 Preheat oven to 400°F. Mist every other cup of a 12-cup muffin tin with nonstick cooking spray. Press a tortilla into each sprayed cup, flattening out edges, and bake until golden, about 8 minutes.

2 Divide beans among tostadas, top with salsa and sprinkle with cheese. Return to oven and bake until warmed through, 7 to 10 minutes.

3 Place each tostada on a plate and sprinkle with cilantro. Top with some lettuce and a small dollop of sour cream. Serve with extra salsa, if desired.

PER SERVING (1 TOSTADA):
177 Cal., 8g Fat (5g Sat.), 20mg Chol., 3g Fiber, 8g Pro., 20g Carb., 440mg Sod.

SMART TIPS

❋ **Watch the portions.** For small appetites, one tostada will be plenty. For bigger kids and adults, two should be just right for dinner.

❋ **Be flexible.** If the tortillas are too stiff to fit inside the muffin tin, place them between two paper towels and microwave them for 10 to 20 seconds to make them more pliable. Work quickly or they'll stiffen up again.

❋ **Make it festive.** Whip up a simple guacamole by mashing two ripe avocados (when choosing them, make sure they give slightly when squeezed) with 1 teaspoon fresh lemon or lime juice and ½ cup chopped red onion. Season well with salt and pepper.

❋ **Spice up your salsa.** Most stores carry an array of salsas, so mix it up. Salsa verde is a delicious mild choice, or try a sweet and spicy pineapple variety.

PREP AN AVOCADO WITH EASE

Learn the best way to get heart-healthy avocados out of their skins and into your favorite dishes.

1 **Give it a twist.** Using a sharp knife, cut the fruit (but not the pit) in half lengthwise. Then gently rotate the halves and separate.

2 **Remove the pit.** Gently penetrate the pit with your knife, taking care not to stab it too hard. Twist the avocado, then lift up the knife—the pit will come right out.

3 **Spoon it out.** Scrape along the inside of the skin with a spoon to get the flesh out. If you aren't using the avocado right away, sprinkle it with lemon juice to prevent browning.

CHARLES SCHILLER; FOOD STYLING: LYNN MILLER (4)

CHICKEN & TURKEY

BEEF & LAMB

PORK

FISH

VEGETABLES

Weeknight Ravioli Lasagna

Prep: 10 min.
Bake: 40 min.
Serves: 4
Cost per serving:

$2.15

- 1¼ cups marinara sauce
- 1 20-oz. package refrigerated cheese ravioli
- 1 10-oz. box frozen chopped spinach, thawed and squeezed dry
- 8 oz. shredded part-skim mozzarella
- ¼ cup grated Parmesan

1 Preheat oven to 375°F. Lightly grease an 8-inch-square baking dish. Spoon ¼ cup marinara sauce over bottom of dish. Cover with half of ravioli. Spread half of remaining sauce over ravioli. Sprinkle on spinach and half of mozzarella. Repeat with remaining ravioli, marinara and mozzarella. Sprinkle top with Parmesan.

2 Cover dish with foil and bake for 30 minutes. Remove foil and bake until bubbling, about 10 minutes longer. Let cool for about 5 minutes before slicing.

PER SERVING: 539 Cal., 22g Fat (12g Sat.), 100mg Chol., 7g Fiber, 33g Pro., 51g Carb., 1,077mg Sod.

Broccoli-Orzo Salad

SMART TIPS

✳ **Waste not.** Instead of using just the broccoli florets, trim, peel and slice the stems, too (they have a clean, fresh, mild flavor and a bit of crunch). Cook them along with the florets and toss into the salad. They're also delicious raw.

✳ **Try a different pasta.** Can't find orzo? Make this tasty salad with elbow macaroni instead.

Prep: 25 min.
Cook: 12 min.
Serves: 8
Cost per serving:

$1.41

- Salt and pepper
- 7 cups chopped broccoli florets (from a 1½-lb. head)
- 1 lb. orzo
- ¼ cup freshly squeezed lemon juice (from 2 medium lemons)
- 1 tsp. grated lemon zest
- ½ tsp. crushed red pepper
- ½ cup extra-virgin olive oil
- 1 cup chopped jarred roasted red peppers
- ½ cup chopped pitted kalamata olives
- 1 15-oz. can cannellini beans, drained and rinsed
- 1 cup grated Parmesan
- ½ cup packed basil leaves, coarsely chopped

1 Bring a large pot of salted water to a boil. Add broccoli florets and cook until bright green and just tender, about 3 minutes. Remove broccoli with a slotted spoon to a colander and run under cold water to stop cooking. Drain well and set aside.

2 Add orzo to same pot of boiling water and cook until al dente, about 9 minutes. While orzo is cooking, whisk lemon juice, zest, crushed red pepper and olive oil in a small bowl. Drain orzo well and transfer to a large serving bowl. Add broccoli, peppers, olives and beans. Pour dressing over orzo mixture and toss to coat completely; set aside to cool to room temperature. When pasta has cooled, toss in cheese and basil. Season with salt and pepper.

PER SERVING: 467 Cal., 20g Fat (4g Sat.), 11mg Chol., 7g Fiber, 17g Pro., 58g Carb., 416 mg Sod.

CHICKEN &
TURKEY

BEEF &
LAMB

PORK

FISH

VEGETABLES

SMART TIPS

✳ **Vary the flavors.**
Substitute sautéed mushrooms or green peas for the olives. For more color and a fresh taste, toss in a handful of chopped fresh herbs such as basil or parsley.

✳ **Swap pastas.**
If you don't care for spinach pasta, use regular penne, or try whole wheat.

Pasta with Cauliflower and Olives

Prep: 10 min.
Cook: 20 min.
Serves: 6
Cost per serving:

$1.54

- 3 cups cauliflower florets, from half a medium head (about 1½ lb.)
- 1 Tbsp. olive oil
- Salt and pepper
- 1 lb. green (spinach) penne
- 1 cup pitted black olives, sliced
- 1 28-oz. jar marinara sauce
- ½ cup grated Parmesan

1 Preheat oven to 450°F. Toss cauliflower with olive oil on a large baking sheet and season with salt and pepper. Roast, stirring and shaking pan once or twice, until cauliflower is lightly browned, 15 to 20 minutes.

2 Bring a large pot of salted water to a boil and add pasta. Cook according to package directions or until al dente, 8 to 10 minutes. Drain thoroughly in a colander. Return pasta to pot.

3 Add olives, marinara sauce and cauliflower to pasta in pot. Sprinkle about ¼ cup Parmesan over pasta and toss. Serve with remaining Parmesan for topping.
PER SERVING: 447 Cal., 14g Fat (4g Sat.), 55mg Chol., 5g Fiber, 17g Pro., 64g Carb., 852mg Sod.

Chili-Cheese Biscuit Pies

Prep: 15 min.
Bake: 10 min.
Serves: 4
Cost per serving:
$1.07

- 2 Tbsp. olive oil
- 1 small onion, diced
- 1 14-oz. can crushed tomatoes, with juices
- 1 15-oz. can red kidney beans, rinsed and drained
- 2 tsp. chili powder
- Salt
- 2 cups instant biscuit mix (such as Bisquick)
- ½ cup milk
- 1 cup grated Cheddar

1 Preheat oven to 450°F. Lightly grease 8 muffin cups or place a foil liner in each.

2 In a medium saucepan, warm oil over medium-high heat and sauté onion until softened and translucent, 3 to 5 minutes. Stir in tomatoes, beans and chili powder and bring to a boil. Reduce heat to medium-low and simmer until chili mixture is slightly thickened, about 5 minutes. Season with salt.

3 While chili is cooking, combine biscuit mix and milk in a medium bowl to form a dough. Turn out onto a lightly floured work surface and pat into a 6-by-9-inch rectangle. Cut into 8 squares with a sharp knife and put each square into a muffin-tin cup, pressing down gently into bottom and pushing slightly up sides of each cup.

4 Scoop about ¼ cup chili into each cup. Sprinkle each with cheese. Bake until chili and cheese are bubbling and biscuits are golden and firm, about 10 minutes.
PER SERVING: 537 Cal., 28g Fat (10g Sat.), 34mg Chol., 8g Fiber, 19g Pro., 58g Carb., 1,667mg Sod.

SMART TIP

✴ **Use a different pan.** Instead of a muffin tin, bake these little pies in ramekins or glass custard cups that go directly from oven to plate.

RYAN BENYI, FOOD STYLING: LYNN MILLER

Pasta with Tomatoes and Mozzarella

Prep: 5 min.
Cook: 15 min.
Serves: 4
Cost per serving:

$2.31

- 1 lb. bow-tie pasta
- 1 pint cherry tomatoes, each cut in half
- ½ cup prepared pesto
- 8 oz. fresh mozzarella, cut into pieces
- ¼ cup olive oil
- Salt and pepper
- ½ cup torn fresh basil
- ¼ cup grated Parmesan

1 Prepare pasta according to package directions, undercooking by 1 minute. Drain pasta and return to pot. Add tomatoes, pesto, mozzarella and olive oil. Season with salt and pepper.

2 Mix well, cover and set aside off heat until cheese has started to melt, about 2 minutes. Stir in basil and Parmesan. Serve immediately.

PER SERVING: 742 Cal., 30g Fat (11g Sat.), 50mg Chol., 5g Fiber, 30g Pro., 88g Carb., 750mg Sod.

SMART TIPS

* **Add ingredients.** Toss in green peas or sautéed zucchini. Want meat? Stir in cooked chopped sausage, ham or chicken.

* **Make it a meal.** Offer a green salad and bread with the pasta. Or serve smaller portions and make it a side dish to go with roasted chicken.

* **Use another pasta.** Any short pasta shape works well with this dish. Try penne, fusilli or orecchiette ("little ears" in Italian).

* **Indulge in the sauce.** To make this dish a decadent treat, stir a bit of heavy cream into the pesto before tossing it with the pasta.

* **Up the fiber.** Boost the meal's fiber and vitamin content with whole-wheat pasta. If your family balks at the whole-wheat variety, try a blend of whole-wheat and regular pasta.

PEEL TOMATOES EFFORTLESSLY

Follow these simple steps to get the delicate skins off tomatoes in a flash.

1 **Make the cut.** Using a sharp paring knife, cut a small X in the bottom of each tomato. Take care not to cut too deeply into the flesh.

2 **Heat up, cool off.** Drop the tomatoes, up to 3 at a time, into a pot of boiling water. After 10 seconds, scoop them out with a slotted spoon and plunge them into a bowl of ice water to stop them from cooking.

3 **Peel away.** When the tomatoes are cool, use a paring knife or your fingers to carefully remove the skins.

Slow-Cooker Eggplant and Tomato Sauce with Pasta

Prep: 10 min.
Cook: 7 hr.
Serves: 6
Cost per serving:
$1.43

- **1 28-oz. can diced tomatoes, drained**
- **1 6-oz. can tomato paste**
- **½ cup red wine or water**
- **1 medium eggplant (about 1 lb.), cut into ½-inch cubes**
- **1 onion, finely chopped**
- **2 cloves garlic, finely chopped**
- **1 tsp. dried oregano**
- **Salt**
- **1 lb. fusilli or other curly pasta**

1 Combine tomatoes, tomato paste, wine or water, eggplant, onion, garlic, oregano and ½ tsp. salt in slow cooker. Cover and cook on low until eggplant is soft and sauce is thick, 5 to 7 hours.

2 Just before sauce is done, bring a large pot of salted water to boil over high heat. Add pasta and cook until al dente, 7 to 10 minutes. Drain pasta, toss with sauce and serve.

PER SERVING: 376 Cal., 2g Fat (0g Sat.), 0mg Chol., 7g Fiber, 13g Pro., 77g Carb., 697mg Sod.

RYAN BENYI, FOOD STYLING: STEPHANA BOTTOM

Corn, Black Bean and Pepper-Jack Burritos

SMART TIPS

Keep it fresh. If fresh corn is in season, swap it in. To get 1 cup, cut the kernels off 2 ears. Cook it as you would the frozen corn.

Add a kick. For a bit of heat, seed and chop a small jalapeño chili. Stir it in while cooking the onion.

Change cheeses. Try these burritos with Cheddar, or a combination.

Prep: 10 min.

Cook: 10 min.

Serves: 4

Cost per serving:

$1.83

- 4 10-inch whole-wheat tortillas
- 2 tsp. vegetable oil
- 1 small onion, chopped
- 1 14-oz. can black beans, rinsed and drained
- 1 cup frozen corn kernels
- 1 cup cherry tomatoes, halved
- 1 Tbsp. lime juice
- Salt
- 6 oz. low-fat pepper Jack, shredded

1 Preheat oven to 300°F. Wrap tortillas in foil and heat until warm and soft, about 10 minutes. Remove from oven and keep wrapped until ready to use.

2 While tortillas are heating, warm vegetable oil in a medium skillet over medium heat. Add onion and cook, stirring frequently, until softened, 3 to 5 minutes. Stir in black beans, corn and cherry tomatoes and cook, stirring often, until completely heated through, about 5 minutes. Stir in lime juice. Season with salt.

3 Place a tortilla on counter. Spoon ¼ of filling along center of tortilla. Sprinkle with ¼ of cheese. Fold sides of tortilla in over filling, then roll up to enclose. Repeat with remaining tortillas, filling and cheese. Cut burritos in half on diagonal. Serve immediately.

PER SERVING: 426 Cal., 19g Fat (7g Sat.), 30mg Chol., 11g Fiber, 22g Pro., 54g Carb., 1,529mg Sod.

RYAN BENYI, FOOD STYLING: STEPHANA BOTTOM

Spinach-Ricotta Skillet Lasagna

SMART TIPS

✳ **Add some meat.**
This lasagna is a hearty meal, but you can add cooked sausage, sliced ham or ground beef if you like.

✳ **Use your noodle.**
No-bake lasagna noodles save time. But if you prefer regular noodles, cook them as the package directs before using here.

Prep: 15 min.
Cook: 20 min.
Serves: 4
Cost per serving:

$2.19

- 1 cup shredded part-skim mozzarella
- ½ cup grated Parmesan
- ¼ tsp. garlic powder
- Salt and pepper
- Pinch of nutmeg
- 1½ cups ricotta
- 1 large egg

- 1 10-oz. package frozen chopped spinach, thawed and squeezed dry
- 1 14-oz. jar tomato sauce
- 4 oz. no-boil lasagna noodles (about half a box)

1 In a medium bowl, mix mozzarella, Parmesan, garlic powder, ¼ tsp. pepper and a pinch of nutmeg. In a separate bowl, whisk ricotta with egg and spinach until blended and smooth. Season with salt and pepper.

2 Spread ⅓ of sauce over bottom of a large, heavy skillet. Arrange 2 pasta sheets on top. Spread half of spinach mixture over pasta, then scatter ⅓ of mozzarella mixture on top. Top with 2 more pasta sheets, then spread with ⅓ of sauce. Sprinkle with ⅓ of mozzarella mixture. Place another 2 sheets on top and pour over remaining sauce. Break remaining sheets of pasta into large pieces

and use them to fill in around edges of skillet.

3 Dollop remaining spinach mixture over top, and sprinkle on remaining mozzarella mixture. Transfer skillet to stovetop and cook, covered, over medium-low heat until top is firm, about 20 minutes. Remove from heat and set aside, covered, for 5 to 10 minutes before serving.

PER SERVING: 485 Cal., 24g Fat (14g Sat.), 126mg Chol., 5g Fiber, 32g Pro., 37g Carb., 791mg Sod.

CHARLES SCHILLER, FOOD STYLING: STEPHANA BOTTOM

Black Bean Burgers

Prep: 10 min.
Bake: 20 min.
Serves: 4
Cost per serving:

67¢

- 2 Tbsp. vegetable oil
- 1 stalk celery, chopped
- 1 onion, finely chopped
- 1 clove garlic, minced
- 1 15-oz. can black beans, rinsed and drained
- 1 large egg, lightly beaten
- 1 Tbsp. cumin
- ½ cup plain bread crumbs
- Salt and pepper

1 Preheat oven to 375°F; lightly grease a large, rimmed baking sheet.

2 Warm oil in a large skillet over medium-high heat. Add celery and onion and cook, stirring often, until softened, 3 to 5 minutes. Add garlic and sauté 1 minute longer.

3 Pour beans into a large bowl and use a fork or potato masher to mash into a thick paste. Scrape vegetables from skillet into bowl. Stir in egg and bread crumbs. Season with salt and pepper. Use your fingers to form into

4 patties (do not overmix). Place patties on baking sheet and bake until firm and set, about 10 minutes on each side. Serve on whole-grain buns with lettuce, tomato and sliced red onion, if desired.

PER SERVING: 215 Cal., 9g Fat (1g Sat.), 53mg Chol., 7g Fiber, 8g Pro., 28g Carb., 821mg Sod.

RYAN BENYI; FOOD STYLING: ANDREA STEINBERG

Pasta with Yogurt Pesto

Prep: 5 min.
Cook: 10 min.
Serves: 4
Cost per serving:

$1.60

- 1 clove garlic, coarsely chopped
- 2 cups tightly packed fresh basil leaves
- ¼ cup walnut pieces or pine nuts
- ⅓ cup extra-virgin olive oil
- ¼ cup grated Parmesan
- ½ cup plain low-fat yogurt
- Salt and pepper
- 1 lb. fusilli or other short, curly pasta

1 Combine garlic, basil and nuts in bowl of a food processor or a blender and process until finely chopped. With motor running, add olive oil in a slow, steady stream. Scrape mixture into a small bowl and stir in cheese and yogurt. Season with salt. Cover with plastic and refrigerate for up to 3 days, until ready to use.

2 Bring a large pot of salted water to a boil and cook pasta until al dente, 7 to 10 minutes. Reserve ½ cup cooking liquid. Drain pasta and return to pot. Toss with pesto. If pasta looks too dry, add reserved cooking liquid, 1 Tbsp. at a time, to moisten. Season with salt and pepper to taste. Serve immediately.

PER SERVING: 709 Cal., 30g Fat (5g Sat.), 8mg Chol., 12g Fiber, 22g Pro., 88g Carb., 386mg Sod.

SMART TIPS

✳ **Use it in other recipes.** This sauce is also good as a dip for vegetables and on top of baked potatoes.

✳ **Go Greek.** For a richer, creamier texture, use plain low-fat Greek yogurt instead of regular.

Spinach-and-Cheese Quiche

Prep: 15 min.
Bake: 45 min.
Serves: 8
Cost per serving:

93¢

- 1 Tbsp. unsalted butter
- ½ onion, finely chopped
- 1 clove garlic, minced
- 1 10-oz. package frozen chopped spinach, thawed and squeezed dry
- 1½ cups grated Gruyère
- 1 9-inch unbaked pie shell
- 3 large eggs, lightly beaten
- 1½ cups milk
- Salt and pepper
- Pinch of nutmeg

1 Preheat oven to 375°F. In a small skillet over medium heat, melt butter. Add onion and sauté until translucent, about 5 minutes. Add garlic and cook for 1 minute longer, stirring. Transfer to a small bowl and let cool.

2 Sprinkle onion mixture, spinach and Gruyère over bottom of pie shell. Beat eggs and milk together, season with salt, pepper and nutmeg. Gently pour into crust.

3 Bake quiche until set and nicely

browned, 40 to 45 minutes. Remove from oven and let rest for 10 minutes.

PER SERVING: 248 Cal., 17g Fat (8g Sat.), 112mg Chol., 2g Fiber, 12g Pro., 13g Carb., 401mg Sod.

Quick Mushroom-Barley Soup

Prep: 10 min.
Cook: 45 min.
Serves: 4
Cost per serving:

$1.55

- 2 Tbsp. vegetable oil
- 1 onion, finely chopped
- 2 carrots, cut into ¼-inch-thick rounds
- 10 oz. white or cremini mushrooms, sliced
- 1 cup pearl barley
- ½ tsp. dried oregano
- ½ tsp. dried thyme
- 3 cups low-sodium chicken broth
- Salt and pepper

1 Warm oil in a large saucepan over medium heat. Add onion and carrots and cook, stirring occasionally, until softened, about 8 minutes. Add mushrooms and sauté until they release their liquid, about 5 minutes. Add barley, oregano and thyme and stir 1 minute.

2 Add chicken broth and 3 cups water and bring to a boil. Lower heat, cover and simmer until barley is tender, about 30 minutes. Season with salt and pepper and serve.

PER SERVING: 294 Cal., 8g Fat (1g Sat.), 0mg Chol., 10g Fiber, 10g Pro., 48g Carb., 737mg Sod.

KANA OKADA, FOOD STYLING: SUSAN VAJARANANT

Cavatelli with Spicy Broccoli

SMART TIPS

✳ Keep it meat-free. Use vegetable broth instead of chicken broth to make this dish vegetarian.

✳ Customize it. If you like a milder dish, start with ½ teaspoon crushed red pepper. Keep adding ¼ teaspoon at a time, if needed, to reach the level of heat that works for you.

Prep: 15 min.

Cook: 12 min.

Serves: 6

Cost per serving:

$2.20

- Salt
- 1 lb. cavatelli or small pasta shells
- ¼ cup extra-virgin olive oil
- 1 onion, finely chopped
- 4 large cloves garlic, smashed and peeled
- 1 14-oz. can chicken broth
- ½ to 1 tsp. crushed red pepper
- 6 cups frozen broccoli florets (about 1½ lb.), thawed
- ½ cup finely grated Parmesan, plus more for serving

1 In a large pot of boiling salted water, cook pasta until al dente, 8 to 10 minutes.

2 In a large skillet, warm oil over medium heat. Add onion and garlic and cook, stirring often, until softened, about 5 minutes. Add chicken broth and crushed red pepper and cook, stirring occasionally, until broth is reduced by half and onion is tender, about 4 minutes. Stir in broccoli florets and cook over low heat until warmed through, about 3 minutes.

3 Drain pasta thoroughly in a colander, reserving 1½ cups cooking water. Return pasta to pot. Remove garlic from skillet and discard.

4 Add contents of skillet, ½ tsp. salt and 1 cup pasta cooking liquid to pasta. Toss well to coat pasta. Add more pasta cooking liquid, 1 Tbsp. at a time, to reach desired consistency. Sprinkle with Parmesan and toss again. Serve with additional Parmesan.

PER SERVING: 418 Cal., 14g Fat (3g Sat.), 5mg Chol., 11g Fiber, 18g Pro., 53g Carb., 686mg Sod.

CHARLES SCHILLER, FOOD STYLING, TRACEY SEAMAN

Cheddar-and-Tomato Bread Pudding

Prep: 15 min.
Bake: 50 min.
Serves: 4
Cost per serving:

93¢

- 1 Tbsp. unsalted butter
- 1 small onion, chopped
- 4 oz. piece of baguette (about ⅓ loaf), sliced ⅔ inch thick and then into cubes
- 3 oz. extra-sharp Cheddar, coarsely shredded
- 1 cup grape or cherry tomatoes, halved
- 4 large eggs
- 1½ cups reduced-fat milk
- ¼ tsp. salt
- ¼ tsp. pepper

1 Arrange rack in center of oven and preheat to 350°F. In a medium skillet, melt butter over medium heat. Add onion and cook, stirring occasionally, until softened, about 5 minutes. Transfer to a bowl and set aside.

2 Lightly grease a shallow, 1½-quart baking dish. Layer bread, cheese and tomatoes in dish. Beat eggs, milk, salt and pepper in bowl with cooked onion. Drizzle over bread.

3 Bake bread pudding until top is puffed and golden, about 50 minutes. Let pudding cool for 5 minutes before serving.

PER SERVING: 320 Cal., 17g Fat (10g Sat.), 253mg Chol., 1g Fiber, 16g Pro., 23g Carb., 570mg Sod.

Baked Eggs in Bread Bowls

Prep: 10 min.
Bake: 25 min.
Serves: 8
Cost per serving:

54¢

- 8 crusty dinner rolls
- 8 large eggs
- ¼ cup chopped mixed herbs such as tarragon, chives and parsley
- 2 Tbsp. heavy cream
- Salt and pepper
- 4 Tbsp. grated Parmesan

1 Preheat oven to 350°F. Slice off top of each dinner roll and, using your fingers, gently remove some of bread until you have a hole large enough to accommodate an egg. Arrange rolls on a rimmed baking sheet. Reserve caps.

2 Crack an egg into each roll, then top with some herbs, a drizzle of cream and a generous sprinkling of salt and pepper. Sprinkle each with Parmesan.

3 Bake until eggs are set and bread is toasted, 20 to 25 minutes. Place caps alongside rolls on baking sheet for the final 5 minutes, until golden brown. Remove from oven and let sit 5 minutes. Top rolls with caps and serve warm.

PER SERVING: 191 Cal., 9g Fat (3g Sat.), 219mg Chol., 1g Fiber, 12g Pro., 18g Carb., 465mg Sod.

Tacos with Sweet Potatoes and Pinto Beans

Prep: 10 min.
Cook: 20 min.
Serves: 4
Cost per serving:

$1.27

- 2 medium sweet potatoes (6 to 8 oz.), peeled and cut into 1-inch pieces
- Salt and pepper
- 2 Tbsp. vegetable oil
- 1 onion, chopped
- 1 jalapeño chili, seeded and chopped
- 1 15.5-oz. can pinto beans, drained and rinsed
- 8 hard taco shells

1 Place sweet potatoes in a large pan; add enough water to cover by 1 inch. Add ¼ tsp. salt; bring to a boil. Reduce heat to medium-high and cook until tender, about 10 minutes. Drain in a colander.

2 Warm oil in a large skillet over medium-high heat. Cook onion and jalapeño, stirring, until softened, about 5 minutes. Stir in beans. Add sweet potatoes; cook 5 minutes. Season with salt and pepper.

3 Spoon about ½ cup filling into each taco shell; serve immediately. Offer rice, salsa, guacamole, sour cream and sliced scallion on the side if desired.

PER SERVING: 322 Cal., 12g Fat (1g Sat.), 0mg Chol., 10g Fiber, 8g Pro., 51g Carb., 695mg Sod.

Broccoli-Cheese Soup

SMART TIPS

✳ Ham it up. Sprinkle diced cooked ham or bacon into the soup if desired.

✳ Have it your way. This recipe makes 8 cups of soup, enough for 8 portions as a starter or 4 dinner servings.

✳ Make your own croutons. Cut stale bread into cubes, toss with olive oil, salt, pepper and a pinch of cayenne, and bake until crisp.

Prep: 10 min.
Cook: 10 min.
Yield: 2 qt.
Cost per serving:

$2.04

- 4 Tbsp. unsalted butter
- 1 large onion, finely diced
- ¼ cup all-purpose flour
- 4 cups chicken broth
- 6 cups frozen broccoli florets (about 1½ lb.), thawed
- 1½ cups milk, slightly warmed
- 2 cups shredded sharp Cheddar
- 2 cups prepared croutons

1 In a large saucepan, melt butter over medium heat until bubbling. Add onion and cook, stirring occasionally, until softened, about 4 minutes. Add flour and cook for 2 minutes, whisking to make a paste. Gradually whisk in broth and bring mixture to a boil. Add broccoli and cook, stirring often, until tender, about 3 minutes. Remove saucepan from heat.

2 Using a blender, puree broccoli mixture in batches. Transfer pureed batches to a large bowl. When all of soup is pureed, return it to saucepan, place over medium-low heat and bring to a simmer. Gradually whisk in milk and 1 cup cheese. Ladle soup into bowls. Top each serving with croutons and a sprinkling of remaining cheese. Serve hot.

PER SERVING (1 CUP): 272 Cal., 17g Fat (11g Sat.), 52mg Chol., 3g Fiber, 12g Pro., 16g Carb., 927mg Sod.

CHARLES SCHILLER. FOOD STYLING: TRACEY SEAMAN

SMART TIPS

✳ **Make cheese toasts.** Brush slices of Italian bread with oil and broil until golden. Sprinkle grated Parmesan on top, then broil until bubbling.

✳ **Vary the vegetables.** Try frozen baby lima beans or edamame in place of the peas.

✳ **Top it off.** Sprinkle the soup with grated Parmesan if desired. Pass additional cheese on the side.

Pasta-and-Bean Soup

Prep: 5 min.
Cook: 25 min.
Serves: 4
Cost per serving:

$2.03

- Salt
- 2 cups ditalini or small pasta shells
- 2 Tbsp. extra-virgin olive oil
- 1 onion, finely chopped
- 1 clove garlic, finely chopped
- 3 cups tomato sauce
- 2 cups low-sodium vegetable broth or chicken broth
- 1 10-oz. package frozen broccoli florets, thawed and chopped
- 1 10-oz. package frozen peas
- 1 15-oz. can chickpeas, drained and rinsed

1 In a pot of boiling salted water, cook pasta until al dente, about 10 minutes. Drain in a colander.

2 Warm oil in a large saucepan over medium heat. Add onion and cook, stirring often, until softened, about 5 minutes. Add garlic and sauté 1 minute. Stir in tomato sauce, broth, broccoli, peas and chickpeas. Bring to a boil, then cover, reduce heat and simmer gently for 10 minutes. Stir in pasta. Serve with cheese toasts (see instructions above) if desired.

PER SERVING: 372 Cal., 9g Fat (1g Sat.), 0mg Chol., 13g Fiber, 17g Pro., 57g Carb., 1,169mg Sod.

Spinach-and-Ricotta Stuffed Shells

Prep: 20 min.
Bake: 45 min.
Serves: 6
Cost per serving:

$2.24

- **24 jumbo pasta shells**
- **Salt and pepper**
- **1 15-oz. container ricotta**
- **2 cups shredded mozzarella**
- **½ cup shredded Parmesan**
- **1 10-oz. package frozen chopped spinach, thawed and squeezed dry**
- **1 large egg, lightly beaten**
- **1 tsp. Italian seasoning**
- **Pinch of nutmeg**
- **1 26-oz. jar spaghetti sauce**

1 Preheat oven to 375°F. Mist a 9-by-13-inch baking dish with cooking spray. Cook pasta shells in a pot of salted boiling water until al dente, about 10 minutes; drain and let cool. While pasta cooks, in a large bowl, stir together ricotta, 1 cup mozzarella, Parmesan, spinach, egg, salt, pepper, Italian seasoning and nutmeg.

2 Spread ¾ cup spaghetti sauce over bottom of baking dish. Stuff shells with cheese-and-spinach mixture and place in dish. Spoon remaining sauce over shells and sprinkle with remaining 1 cup mozzarella.

3 Cover baking dish with foil and bake for 35 minutes. Remove foil and bake until bubbly and cheese begins to brown, about 10 minutes longer.
PER SERVING: 498 Cal., 26g Fat (13g Sat.), 88mg Chol., 7g Fiber, 28g Pro., 41g Carb., 1,253mg Sod.

SMART TIP

✳ **Don't stick.** Mist foil with cooking spray before covering dish.

Broccoli-and-Feta Frittata

Prep: 5 min.
Cook: 18 min.
Serves: 4
Cost per serving:

$1.80

- 1 Tbsp. unsalted butter
- ½ onion, finely diced
- 2 cups chopped broccoli florets
- Salt and pepper
- 7 large eggs
- 3 oz. feta cheese, crumbled

1 In an 8-inch ovenproof skillet or well-seasoned cast-iron pan, melt butter over medium heat. Add onion and cook, stirring occasionally, until translucent, about 4 minutes. Add broccoli, sprinkle with salt and pepper and cook, stirring occasionally, until just tender, about 6 minutes longer.

2 Preheat broiler to high and place an oven rack 4 to 5 inches from heat source. In a medium bowl, whisk together eggs; season with additional salt and pepper. Pour eggs over onion-broccoli mixture, stir to combine, then dot surface with feta. Cook, without stirring, until eggs are set on bottom and beginning to set on top, about 5 minutes. Transfer skillet to oven and broil until eggs are completely set and just beginning to brown, 2 to 3 minutes. Cut into wedges and serve hot or at room temperature.

PER SERVING: 232 Cal., 16g Fat (8g Sat.), 397mg Chol., 1g Fiber, 16g Pro., 6g Carb., 666mg Sod.

SMART TIPS

✳ **Swap veggies.** You can use spinach instead of broccoli and add a pinch of dried oregano for a Greek flair. Or try another vegetable, such as asparagus, mushrooms or zucchini (be sure to sauté zucchini, mushrooms or spinach first to remove the excess water). If you have leftover cooked vegetables in the fridge, toss them in.

✳ **Take care.** Be sure to use a skillet that's ovenproof, especially since it has to withstand the intense heat of the broiler. If your pan has a plastic or wooden handle, wrap it tightly with foil before broiling.

KNOW YOUR EGGS

Putting eggs in your shopping basket? There are so many to choose from these days. Here's what the different labels mean.

Free-range
People like buying free-range eggs because the hens are raised outside or have regular access to the outdoors. The eggs have the same nutrients as other eggs.

Cage-free
Similar to free-range eggs, these come from hens that are not kept in cages (but may be kept indoors). Cage-free eggs have the same nutrients as regular eggs.

Omega-3-enriched
These eggs come from hens that have been fed a diet rich in ground flaxseed, a grain that contains heart-healthy omega-3 fatty acids, so they're healthier.

Vegetarian
The hens that produce these eggs have been fed grains only—no animal by-products.

Organic
These come from hens whose feed is produced without pesticides, herbicides or commercial fertilizers. These eggs cost more because they're more expensive to produce.

※

SMART TIPS

※ **Add meat.** This is a hearty vegetarian stew, but if you'd like to include meat, stir in chunks of ham, Canadian bacon or cooked chicken toward the end of the cooking time. You also can use low-sodium chicken broth instead of water.

※ **Serve it up.** Rice makes a good accompaniment to this stew, or serve it with whole-grain bread to sop up the juices. For a dinner party, hollow out small crusty bread loaves and use them as bowls for the stew.

Slow-Cooker Peanut–Sweet Potato Stew

Prep: 20 min.
Cook: 5 hr.
Serves: 4
Cost per serving:

$2.01

- 6 small sweet potatoes, peeled, cut crosswise into ¾-inch slices (about 2 lb.)
- 3 red onions, thinly sliced
- 1 14.5-oz. can diced tomatoes
- 5 sprigs plus ½ cup chopped fresh flat-leaf parsley
- 1½ tsp. ground cumin
- ½ tsp. ground allspice
- Salt and pepper
- ½ cup creamy or crunchy peanut butter

1 Stir together sweet potatoes, onions, tomatoes, parsley sprigs, cumin, allspice, salt, pepper and 2 cups water in a slow cooker until thoroughly combined. Cover and cook for 4 to 5 hours on high. Discard parsley sprigs.

2 Just before serving stew, stir in chopped parsley and peanut butter. Serve hot in bowls.

PER SERVING: 318 Cal., 11g Fat (2g Sat.), 0mg Chol., 5g Fiber, 10g Pro., 47g Carb., 529mg Sod.

Vegetable Moussaka

SMART TIP

✳ **DIY and save.**
Greek yogurt, which is strained of excess water to make it thicker, is pricier than regular yogurt. To make your own, line a colander with cheesecloth or paper towels and set in a larger bowl. Spoon plain yogurt into the colander, cover with plastic wrap and refrigerate for a few hours or overnight.

Prep: 45 min.

Bake: 1 hr. 30 min.

Rest: 50 min.

Serves: 8

Cost per serving:

$1.40

- 1 4-lb. eggplant, cut into ½-inch rounds
- Salt and pepper
- ¼ cup plus 2 Tbsp. olive oil
- 1 large onion, chopped
- 10 oz. white mushrooms, sliced
- 1 cup diced zucchini
- 1 cup diced yellow squash
- ¼ cup chopped fresh parsley
- 1 tsp. dried oregano
- 1 28-oz. can crushed tomatoes in puree
- 4 cloves garlic, minced
- ½ cup plus 4 Tbsp. grated Parmesan
- 4 Tbsp. unsalted butter
- 5 Tbsp. all-purpose flour
- 3 cups milk
- 7 oz. Greek yogurt
- 2 large eggs plus 2 large yolks, lightly beaten

1 Preheat oven to 425°F. Lay eggplant slices on paper towels. Sprinkle with salt on both sides; let stand for 30 minutes. Rinse and pat dry. Brush both sides with olive oil (¼ cup total); place on 2 baking sheets. Bake 20 minutes, turning slices and rotating pans halfway through. Remove from oven and let cool. Reduce oven temperature to 350°F.

2 In a large skillet, heat remaining oil. Add onion, mushrooms, zucchini and squash, season with salt and pepper and cook, covered, over low heat until soft, about 10 minutes. Uncover, turn heat to high and cook, stirring, until liquid evaporates. Add parsley, oregano, tomatoes and puree and garlic; cook, stirring often, until sauce has thickened, about 10 minutes.

3 Mist a 13-by-9-inch baking dish with cooking spray. Cover bottom of dish with eggplant rounds, spoon half of vegetable sauce on top and sprinkle with 2 Tbsp. Parmesan. Repeat with remaining eggplant and sauce and 2 Tbsp.

Parmesan, finishing with a top layer of eggplant.

4 Melt butter in pan and whisk in flour. Cook for 2 minutes. Whisk in milk and cook, stirring, until mixture comes to a boil. Reduce heat and simmer until sauce thickens, about 5 minutes. Add yogurt and ½ cup Parmesan and stir until smooth. Whisk in eggs and yolks.

5 Pour cheese sauce over eggplant. Place on a foil-lined baking sheet and bake until heated through and top is browned, about 70 minutes. Let rest for 20 minutes before slicing and serving.

PER SERVING: 437 Cal., 28g Fat (12g Sat.), 151mg Chol., 11g Fiber, 17g Pro., 34g Carb., 720mg Sod.

Index

A

Ancho Chili–Rubbed Flank Steak, *74*

Apricot-Onion Pork Medallions, *110*

Asian Sesame Noodles with Chicken, *41*

B

Bacon-and-Pea-Stuffed Potatoes, *114*

Baked Eggs in Bread Bowls, *163*

Baked Pasta Primavera, *139*

Baked Potatoes Stuffed with Turkey, Bacon and Cheddar, *45*

Baked Ziti with Broccoli and Sausage, *89*

Balsamic-Marinated Flank Steak, *70*

Barbecued Pork Sliders, *103*

Beef and Barley Soup, *65*

Beef-and-Pasta Casserole, *59*

Beef-and-Rice-Stuffed Peppers, *67*

Beef Kebabs with Orange Glaze, *63*

Beer Can Chicken, *45*

Black Bean Burgers, *157*

Black Bean Soup with Sausage, *117*

Braised Chicken with Potatoes, *25*

Braised Pork Chops with Apples and Onion, *93*

Broccoli-and-Cheddar Mini Quiches, *145*

Broccoli and Double Cheese Calzones, *142*

Broccoli-and-Feta Frittata, *169*

Broccoli-Cheese Soup, *165*

Broccoli-Orzo Salad, *149*

Buttermilk Chicken Tenders, *52*

Butternut Squash Ravioli with Pancetta, *84*

C

Caribbean Jerk Chicken, *14*

Cavatelli with Spicy Broccoli, *161*

Cheddar-and-Tomato Bread Pudding, *163*

Cheesy Baked Penne with Ham and Broccoli, *123*

Cheesy Chicken Taco Casserole, *12*

Cheesy Twice-Baked Potatoes, *43*

Chicken Breasts with Peppers, *33*

Chicken Burritos, *32*

Chicken Fried Rice with Vegetables, *53*

Chicken Piccata, *23*

Chicken Salad Club Sandwiches, *23*

Chicken Sausages with Beans, *29*

Chicken Thighs with Mustard-Citrus Sauce, *41*

Chicken Thighs with Spicy Peanut Sauce, *7*

Chicken with Herbed Dumplings, *15*

Chicken with Tomatoes and Arugula, *37*

Chili-Cheese Biscuit Pies, *151*

Chili-Lime Pork Tenderloin, *96*

Cider-Braised Pork Medallions, *107*

Cincinnati Chili, *73*

Coconut Shrimp and Rice, *128*

Coffee-Brined Chicken Drumsticks, *35*

Corn and Cheese Enchiladas, *136*

Corn, Black Bean and Pepper-Jack Burritos, *155*

Corned Beef and Cabbage, *62*

Corn Flake–Crusted Chicken, *26*

Creamy Chicken and Broccoli Curry, *51*

Creamy Corn Chowder, *111*

Crispy Ravioli, *141*

Crunchy Pecan-Crusted Chicken Fingers, *51*

Curried Chicken and Chickpea Stew, *48*

Curried Lamb Stew with Carrots, *80*

E

Easy Broiled Drumsticks, *8*

Easy Spaghetti and Meatballs, *77*

F

Fish Stick Tacos, *127*

French Bread Pizzas, *42*

Fried Brown Rice with Broccoli and Tofu, *141*

Fried Rice with Ham and Asparagus, *104*

G

Grilled Chicken, Peach and Arugula Salad, *29*

Grilled Chicken Quesadillas, *13*

Grilled Turkey, Cheddar and Apple Sandwiches, *36*

H

Ham and Cheddar Supper Waffles, *102*

Ham and Gruyère Stratas, *120*

Ham, Swiss and Spinach Quiche, *119*

Hearty Minestrone with Shells, *123*

Herb-Parmesan Chicken Breasts, *6*

Honey-Mustard Ham Steaks, *92*

I

Italian Tuna Melts, *131*

L

Lamb Chops with Tahini Sauce, *79*

Lemon-Herb Chicken Thighs, *24*

Lemon-Rosemary Chicken, 11

Lemony Chicken Breasts with Rice, 47

M

Maple-Glazed Ham Steak, 90

Maple-Glazed Salmon Fillets, 127

Meat Loaf with Mozzarella, Mushrooms and Pepperoni, 64

Mediterranean Brisket, 81

Mini Meat Loaves, 68

Molasses-and-Mustard-Glazed Ribs, 108

Monte Cristo Sandwiches, 99

N

Niçoise Pasta Salad, 133

O

Orange Beef and Broccoli Stir-Fry, 57

Oven-Baked Mexican Meatballs, 56

P

Parmesan Pork Cutlets, 98

Pasta-and-Bean Soup, 166

Pasta Carbonara Frittata, 116

Pasta with Cauliflower and Olives, 150

Pasta with Chicken and Artichokes, 31

Pasta with Chickpeas and Broccoli, 143

Pasta with Ricotta and Edamame, 144

Pasta with Tomatoes and Mozzarella, 153

Pasta with Yogurt Pesto, 159

Pea Pancakes with Bacon, 89

Penne with Ham and Asparagus, 86

Penne with Sweet Peas and Prosciutto, 101

Pita Bread and Pea Salad, 138

Pork and Hominy Stew, 91

Pork and Peanut Stir-Fry, 119

Pork Chops with Rhubarb Chutney, 87

Q

Quick Mushroom-Barley Soup, 160

R

Refried Bean Tostadas, 147

Rice Noodles with Beef, 69

Ricotta-and-Ham-Stuffed Chicken Breasts, 17

Risotto with Turkey Sausage, 38

Roast Beef and Romaine Salad, 61

S

Salami and Swiss Hoagies, 101

Sautéed Chickpeas with Broccoli and Parmesan, 137

Sirloin Burgers with Mushroom Cream Sauce, 76

Skillet Chicken Parmesan, 46

Skirt Steak with Chimichurri, 61

Slow-Cooker Barbecue Turkey Meatballs, 9

Slow-Cooker Eggplant and Tomato Sauce with Pasta, 154

Slow-Cooker Peanut–Sweet Potato Stew, 170

Slow-Cooker Pulled Pork, 85

Slow-Cooker Shepherd's Pie, 75

Soy-Marinated Pork Chops, 95

Spicy Chicken Stew, 11

Spinach-and-Cheese Quiche, 159

Spinach-and-Ricotta Stuffed Shells, 167

Spinach-Ricotta Skillet Lasagna, 156

Spinach Salad with Chickpeas and Warm Bacon Vinaigrette, 115

Stuffed Smoked Pork Chops, 105

Stuffed Summer Squash, 39

Sweet-and-Sour Brisket, 58

T

Tacos with Sweet Potatoes and Pinto Beans, 164

Tandoori Roasted Pork Tenderloin, 121

Teriyaki Chicken Drumsticks, 18

Thai-Marinated Broiled Flank Steak, 73

Three-Bean Chili with Bacon, 107

Tortellini Salad with Salmon and Peas, 130

Tortellini with Ham and Peas, 97

Tortilla Pie, 71

Tortilla Soup, 49

Tuna Noodle Casserole, 129

Turkey Cutlets with Fresh Corn, 21

Turkey Meatballs, 27

Turkey Nachos, 30

Turkey Reubens, 19

V

Vegetable Moussaka, 171

W

Weeknight Ravioli Lasagna, 148

Western Frittata, 113

White Bean and Chicken Chili, 20

White Bean Soup, 109

all*you

Editor Clare McHugh
Design Director Brenda E. Angelilli
Executive Editor Susan Spencer
Managing Editor George Kimmerling
Food Editor Beth Lipton
Style Editor Carole Nicksin
Photo Editor Mercedes Vizcaino
Associate Editor (Food) Jayna Maleri
Designer Danielle Avraham
Assistant Managing Editor Jamie Roth Major
Copy Chief Caryn Prime
Copy Editors Mark Yawdoszyn, Ali Bahrampour
Senior Editor (Style) Elizabeth Blake

Publisher Diane Oshin (212-522-9879)
Associate Publisher, Marketing Suzanne Quint
Business Office Regina Buckley (Vice President, Finance)
Time Inc. Lifestyle Group Steve Sachs (President)

Publisher Richard Fraiman
General Manager Steven Sandonato
Executive Director, Marketing Services Carol Pittard
Director, Retail & Special Sales Tom Mifsud
Director, New Product Development Peter Harper
Assistant Director, Bookazine Marketing Laura Adam
Assistant Publishing Director, Brand Marketing Joy Butts
Associate Counsel Helen Wan
Design & Prepress Manager Anne-Michelle Gallero
Book Production Manager Susan Chodakiewicz
Associate Manager, Product Marketing Nina Fleishman

SPECIAL THANKS: Christine Austin, Glenn Buonocore, Jim Childs,
Rose Cirrincione, Jacqueline Fitzgerald, Lauren Hall, Jennifer Jacobs,
Suzanne Janso, Brynn Joyce, Mona Li, Robert Marasco, Amy Migliaccio,
Brooke Reger, Dave Rozzelle, Ilene Schreider, Adriana Tierno,
Alex Voznesenskiy, Sydney Webber

ISBN 13: 978-1-60320-849-9
ISBN 10: 1-60320-849-6

ALL YOU Books is a trademark of Time Inc. We welcome your comments and suggestions about ALL YOU Books.
Please write to us at: ALL YOU Books, Attention: Book Editors, PO Box 11016, Des Moines, IA 50336-1016.

If you would like to order any of our hardcover Collector's Edition books, please call us at 800-327-6388
(7 a.m. to 8 p.m. Monday through Friday or 7 a.m. to 6 p.m. Saturday, Central Time).